Historic Dalkeith

the archaeological implications of development

E Patricia **Dennison**

Russel **Coleman**

the Scottish burgh survey

HISTORIC SCOTLAND

in association with

SCOTTISH CULTURAL PRESS

Midlothian

CENTRE FOR SCOTTISH URBAN HISTORY
Department of Scottish History
University of Edinburgh

THE UNIVERSITY OF EDINBURGH

publication	Historic Scotland *in association with* Scottish Cultural Press First published 1998
copyright	© Historic Scotland 1998 *The moral right of the authors has been asserted.*
editorial	Olwyn Owen
design	Christina Unwin
printing . binding	British Printing Company, Aberdeen
ISSN	1358 0272
Scottish Cultural Press ISBN	1 898218 50 1
all distribution and sales enquiries Scottish burgh survey	Scottish Cultural Press Unit 14 . Leith Walk Business Centre 130 Leith Walk Edinburgh EH6 5DT telephone *0131* 555 5950 . facsimile *0131* 555 5018
all other enquiries	■ Scottish burgh surveys Centre for Scottish Urban History Department of Scottish History University of Edinburgh EH8 9LN telephone *0131* 650 4032 . facsimile *0131* 650 4032 ■ Historic Scotland Longmore House Salisbury Place Edinburgh EH9 1SH telephone *0131* 668 8600 . facsimile *0131* 668 8699
British Library cataloguing in publication data	A catalogue record for this book is available from the British Library

All rights are reserved.
No part of this publication
may be reproduced,
stored in a retrieval system,
transmitted or utilised
in any form or by any means
electronic, mechanical
or by photocopying,
recording or otherwise,
without the written permission
of Historic Scotland
and the Scottish Cultural Press.

contents

figures

APS	*The Acts of the Parliaments of Scotland*, edd T Thomson & C Innes (Edinburgh, 1814–75).
CDS	*Calendar of Documents Relating to Scotland*, edd J Bain *et al* (Edinburgh, 1881–1969).
CSP Scot	*Calendar of State Papers Relating to Scotland and Mary, Queen of Scots*, edd J Bain *et al* (Edinburgh, 1898–1967).
Cowan & Easson	*Medieval Religious Houses: Scotland*, edd I B Cowan & D E Easson (Glasgow, 1964).
DES	*Discovery and Excavation in Scotland.*
Edin Recs	*Extracts from the Records of the Burgh of Edinburgh*, edd J D Marwick *et al* (SBRS, 1871–1967).
ER	*The Exchequer Rolls of Scotland*, edd J Stuart *et al* (Edinburgh, 1878–).
Glas Arch Jour	*Glasgow Archaeological Journal.*
Groome	*Ordnance Gazetteer of Scotland*, ed Francis Groome (Edinburgh, 1886).
NMRS	National Monuments Record of Scotland.
NSA	*The New Statistical Account of Scotland* (Edinburgh, 1845).
OSA	*The Statistical Account of Scotland, 1791–1799*, ed Sir John Sinclair. New Edition, edd I R Grant & D J Withrington (Wakefield, 1973).
PSAS	*Proceedings of the Society of Antiquaries of Scotland.*
RCAHMS	Royal Commission on the Ancient and Historical Monuments of Scotland.
RCRB	*Extracts from the Records of the Convention of Royal Burghs of Scotland*, ed J D Marwick (SBRS, 1870–1918).
RMS	*The Register of the Great Seal of Scotland*, edd J M Thomson *et al* (Edinburgh, 1882–1914).
RPC	*The Register of the Privy Council of Scotland*, edd J H Burton *et al* (Edinburgh, 1877–).
RRS	*Regesta Regum Scottorum 1153-1406*, edd G W S Barrow *et al* (Edinburgh, 1960–).
RSMC(D)	Robert Smith Memorial Committee (Dalkeith).
RSS	*Register of the Privy Seal of Scotland (Registrum Secreti Sigilli Regum Scotorum)*, edd M Livingstone *et al* (Edinburgh, 1908).
SBRS	Scottish Burgh Records Society.
SHS	Scottish History Society.
SRO	Scottish Record Office, Edinburgh.
SUAT	Scottish Urban Archaeological Trust.
TA	*Accounts of the Lord High Treasurer of Scotland*, edd T Dickson *et al* (Edinburgh, 1877–).

acknowledgements

The Centre for Scottish Urban History is indebted to a number of people for their assistance and advice.

Especial thanks go to **the people of Dalkeith**, who were consistently welcoming and helpful. Ms Janice Winning, **Scottish Natural Heritage (Dalkeith Office)**, and Mr Cameron Manson, **Dalkeith Country Park Ranger Service**, were very helpful.

We are grateful to Dr David Caldwell of the **National Museums of Scotland** for his valuable comments on Dalkeith's medieval finds. The **Royal Commission on the Ancient and Historical Monuments of Scotland** has been particularly supportive, as have staff of **Historic Scotland**. The staff of the **Scottish Record Office** and of the **National Library of Scotland**, at both George IV Bridge and the Map Library at Causewayside, have been very helpful. The staff of **Edinburgh City Libraries** and **Edinburgh University Library** have also given invaluable assistance.

We appreciate the support of colleagues in the **Department of Scottish History** and in the **Scottish Urban Archaeological Trust**, in particular Ms Catherine Smith.

Editorial assistance was provided by Mrs Melissa Seddon. The index was prepared by Mrs Hilary Flenley. The illustrations were collated by Mr Robin Macpherson.

For permission to reproduce photographs and other illustrations, we wish to thank the following.

figure 3 is reproduced by kind permission of the **Secretary of State for Scotland**. © Crown Copyright.

figures 4, 5, 7, 10, 12, 13 *&* **15–17** are reproduced by kind permission of the **Royal Commission on the Ancient and Historical Monuments of Scotland**. © Crown Copyright: RCAHMS.

figures 6, 8, 9 *&* **14** are reproduced by kind permission of the **Trustees of the National Library of Scotland**.

figures 22 *&* **24** are reproduced by kind permission of the **Trustees of the National Museums of Scotland**.

figures 1, 2, 18–21, 23 *&* **25** are based upon the Ordnance Survey 1:10,000 scale (1991) and the Ordnance Survey 1:2,500 and 1:5,000 map series (1995), with the permission of **The Controller of Her Majesty's Stationery Office**. © Crown Copyright.

figure 11 The source and location of the original *Plan of Dalkeith* drawn by John Lesslie *c* 1770 is unknown, as is the source of a photocopy of an undated tracing of the original—reproduced here as **figure 11**. A photocopy of the probably twentieth-century tracing is held by the National Library of Scotland (Map Library, Causewayside, Edinburgh). The Map Library would be grateful for any information as to the whereabouts of the original or the circumstances of the tracing.

The first mention of Dalkeith occurs *c* 1143 when David I (1124–53) granted land at 'Dolchet' [Dalkeith] to Holyrood Abbey, but there was probably already a castle and settlement here, perhaps in the present Dalkeith Parks. By the end of the fourteenth century, this small settlement had grown sufficiently to be referred to as a 'villa' or town; and it entered an era of increased trade and prosperity when Robert III (1390–1406) granted that James Douglas, the first lord of Dalkeith, could hold it as a free burgh of barony in 1401. Proximity to Edinburgh brought both commercial advantage and disadvantage; Edinburgh needed supplies from the surrounding towns but could, at times, be a somewhat overbearing neighbour. The castle continued to be a focal point throughout these early years of the burgh, and was often the resting place for royalty. By the end of the sixteenth century, the fourth earl had converted it into a 'magnificent palace', remnants of which survive today in Dalkeith House. After the Union of the Crowns in 1603, Dalkeith was to see royalty more rarely. Another change in the old order was the passing of the ownership of Dalkeith to the Buccleuch family in 1642. It was Anne, duchess of Buccleuch, who re-built the family home almost in its entirety in the early eighteenth century, and transformed its grounds with avenues and vistas. The town and palace always remained in relatively close contact, although the erection of the Duke's Gates in 1784, at the head of the High Street, physically defined the separateness of estate and town. By then the population was on the increase and Dalkeith was to progress through the nineteenth and twentieth centuries as a prosperous market town.

Historic Dalkeith is one of a series of reports on the historic burghs of Scotland—known collectively as the *Scottish Burgh Survey*—all of which have been commissioned by **Historic Scotland** and its predecessors. The main aim of the survey is to identify those areas of the present and historic burgh which are of archaeological interest and therefore require sensitive treatment in the event of any proposed development or other ground disturbance. It is designed primarily as a manual for the use of local authorities and archaeological curators. However, as an essential prerequisite to this assessment of the archaeological implications of development, it also describes and illustrates the geography and topography of the town, its known archaeology and history, its historic standing buildings and the origins of its street names—all of which will be of interest to the wider public, be they inhabitant, visitor or student.

Historic Dalkeith was prepared for Historic Scotland within the **Centre for Scottish Urban History**, under the supervision of its Director, Dr E Patricia Dennison. The Centre is part of the Department of Scottish History, University of Edinburgh. Dr Dennison and Mr Russel Coleman, of the **Scottish Urban Archaeological Trust**, are co-authors of the report; Mr Kevin Hicks, of the **Centre for Field Archaeology**, University of Edinburgh, is cartographer and illustrator; and Mr Robin Macpherson of the Scottish History Department acted as Research Assistant. The research team comprised Jim McCormack, Ruth Grant, Sharon Adams and Dean Jacobs, postgraduates in the Department of Scottish History, and Simon Stronach of SUAT. The project is supervised by the Head of the Department of Scottish History, Professor Michael Lynch, and managed for Historic Scotland by Ms Olwyn Owen, Inspector of Ancient Monuments, who is also general editor of the series.

The research on historic Dalkeith was carried out during November and December 1995. This survey was entirely funded by Historic Scotland with help from the Centre for Scottish Urban History. The report has been published with financial assistance from **Midlothian Council** and Historic Scotland. Further copies may be obtained from **Scottish Cultural Press**, Unit 14, Leith Walk Business Centre, 130 Leith Walk, Edinburgh EH6 5DT.

Historic Scotland
September 1997

the Scottish burgh survey

D

how to use this survey

summary

1 **Use the colour-coded map on the foldout at the back of this book figure 25** and/or the **general index** to locate a particular site (normally the site of a development proposal).

2 **Green areas (light and dark green)** are designated as potentially archaeologically sensitive. If the site is in a green area, it is possible that a proposal involving ground disturbance may encounter archaeological remains. Seek appropriate archaeological advice as early as possible.

3 **Red areas** are Scheduled Ancient Monuments or properties in the care of the Secretary of State for Scotland, and are protected by law. Consult Historic Scotland.

4 Use the map on p 48 **figure 18** to determine into which area of the burgh the site falls (Area 1, 2, 3 or 4), and turn to the relevant area in the **area by area assessment** for a fuller account (pp 49–57).

5 Use the **general index** and, if appropriate, the listing of **street names** (pp 91–3) for rapid access to information specific to a site, street or named feature of the town.

step 1

As a working manual, the first point of reference is the colour-coded map on the foldout at the back of the book **figure 25**.

The **red areas** are **protected by law**. Under the provisions of the Ancient Monuments and Archaeological Areas Act 1979 all development proposals which affect them require the prior written consent of the Secretary of State for Scotland (Scheduled Monument Consent) in addition to any planning permission required. These provisions are administered on behalf of the Secretary of State by Historic Scotland. **All applications for planning permission which affect either the site or setting of a Scheduled Ancient Monument (red area) must be referred to Historic Scotland**, acting for the Secretary of State in terms of Section 15(j)(v) of the Town and Country Planning (General Development Procedure) (Scotland) Order 1992 and Section 5(e) of its Amendment (No. 2) Order 1994. *All enquiries regarding prospective development proposals in or adjacent to red areas should be referred to Historic Scotland for advice at as early a stage as possible.*

The **green areas (light and dark green)** are **potentially archaeologically sensitive** and may retain significant sub-surface archaeological information. *Consultation should take place with the local authority planning department, where any development proposal or enquiry involving ground disturbance is being considered*, including car parks, road schemes, environmental improvements, landscaping and drainage schemes, as well as the usual range of development and re-development proposals in built-up areas. There is no necessity for consultation where ground disturbance is not in prospect, such as applications for change of use of a building. There may, however, be a requirement to obtain *planning permission* or, in the case of a listed building, *listed building consent* or, if demolition works are proposed within a conservation area, *conservation area consent*. In such instances, early consultation with the staff of the local authority planning department will always be helpful.

If in doubt whether consultation is necessary, please refer to the local authority archaeologist and the local authority planning department. It is important to note that sub-surface disturbance within historic standing buildings may also affect archaeological remains, and that some standing buildings may retain archaeological features within their structures. Please seek advice as required.

step 2

In this new series of burgh surveys, each survey has been organised locationally, in order to assist speedy consultation on any proposed development site. In the case of Dalkeith, the historic core of the town has been divided into four arbitrary areas, Areas 1 to 4, which are shown on the plan on p 48 **figure 18**. The second step for the user, then, is to consult this plan and to determine into which area a specific enquiry falls.

It should be noted here that Dalkeith lies on a north-east to south-west axis. For the purposes of this study, High Street is discussed as lying on an east–west axis with River North Esk to the north and River South Esk to the south.

step 3

Each area is assessed individually in the **area by area assessment** (pp 49–57). The commentary for each area is prefaced with a detailed plan of that area. Archaeological, historical, geographical and geological factors of particular relevance to the area are all discussed and an assessment of the archaeological potential is made. For ease of reference, even if a dividing line between areas is shown as the middle of a street, discussion of the area includes any elements within the street up to the opposite frontage. The importance of an integrated approach to the historical and archaeological information is implicit in the design of this report: the history and archaeology are presented together on each page rather than consecutively.

This integrated, area-based approach has involved some repetition of information in the area by area assessment, in order that users are not required to cross-reference more than necessary when dealing with a specific enquiry. For instance, the siting, nature and use of the town ports is discussed in all those areas where a port is, or may have been, situated. Although such repetition would not be normal in a work of interest to the general public, it was felt that it would be permissible here in order to facilitate the work of primary users: local authority planners and other curators of the archaeological resource.

historic standing buildings

historic buildings reinforces the above sections by providing basic historical and architectural information about the historic standing buildings of the town; where relevant, it also provides the area location and an assessment of the archaeological potential of specific buildings. *It should always be borne in mind that historic standing buildings may also contain archaeological remains, both beneath their floors and within their structures.* Some of these buildings may be listed and consequently subject to listed building control. Where listed buildings contain, or may contain, architecturally or archaeologically significant building fabric, the planning authority is obliged to make efforts to ensure that this is preserved and not adversely affected by proposed building works.

objectives for future fieldwork and research

Any report of this nature cannot be definitive. During its preparation, a series of archaeological and historical objectives for future fieldwork and research has been identified; these are listed at pp 87–9. They will be of particular interest to urban historians and archaeologists, and to those responsible for management of the archaeological resource in historic Dalkeith.

referencing

The **notes** to the background chapters detail all the documentary and archaeological sources used (*see also* the list of **abbreviations**). The **area by area assessments** are not footnoted separately but references are provided for the previous archaeological work and chance finds listed at the end of each area assessment. The report contains a comprehensive **general index** as well as a listing of **street names** giving basic historical information and, where relevant, area location. A **bibliography** and a **glossary** of technical terms have also been included.

The data accumulated during preparation of this survey and draft copies of the completed work, as well as all unpublished reports of any small-scale excavations and watching briefs, are housed in the **National Monuments Record**, John Sinclair House, 16 Bernard Terrace, Edinburgh EH8 9NX, telephone *0131* 662 1456, facsimile *0131* 662 1477/1499.

full reference to this report

Dennison, E Patricia and Coleman, R 1998 *Historic Dalkeith: the archaeological implications of development*, published by Historic Scotland in association with Scottish Cultural Press, Edinburgh. (Scottish Burgh Survey 1998).

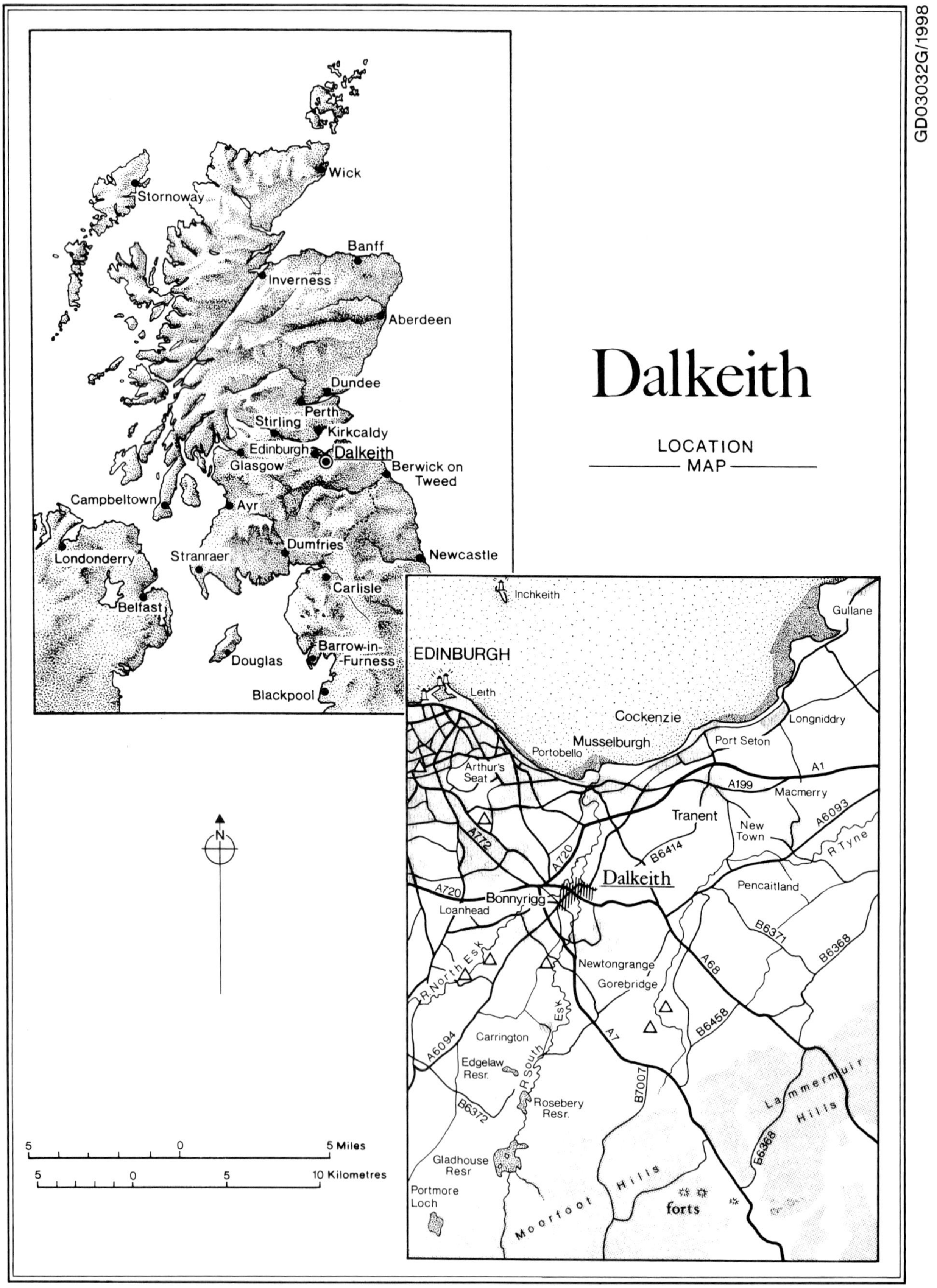

figure 1

Location of Dalkeith

Dalkeith: its site and setting

introduction and location **figure 1**

Dalkeith lies approximately ten kilometres south-east of Edinburgh, in the former county of Midlothian. The historic (medieval) core of the town occupies a narrow wedge of land between two branches of the River Esk, the North and South Esk. The confluence, known as 'The Meeting of the Waters', lies approximately a kilometre and a half to the north-east of Dalkeith, from which point the river continues on to Musselburgh and the sea.

Midlothian is largely hemmed in by high ground. The Pentland Hills form a ridge to the west of Dalkeith, extending almost to the fringes of Edinburgh. To the south lie the Moorfoot and Lammermuir Hills, marking the edge of the Southern Uplands. East of the Pentland Hills, the Lothians stretch uninterruptedly to the North Sea at Dunbar, home to some of the richest agricultural land in the country. Framed by hills, the broad corridor that forms Midlothian, also known as 'the garden of Scotland', is cut by a trio of winding rivers, the North and South Esk and the Tyne. For centuries this has been the commuter belt for Edinburgh, the landscape littered with medieval castles and country houses.[1] From the early eighteenth century bankers, merchants and advocates of Edinburgh had their rural residences here, so much so that the county became known as Edinburghshire.[2] Prior to that, Midlothian was home to some of the finest late medieval architecture in the country, including Crichton Castle and Roslin Chapel.

Before local government reorganisation in 1975, Midlothian was an important county, covering some 82,000 hectares.[3] The Firth of Forth provided a natural boundary to the north, but elsewhere Midlothian bordered seven other counties: West Lothian lay to the west, Lanarkshire, Peeblesshire, Selkirkshire and Roxburghshire to the south and south-west, and Berwickshire and East Lothian to the south and south-east. Edinburgh was the only large town in the county, with smaller burghs such as Bonnyrigg and Lasswade, Loanhead, Musselburgh and Penicuik predominating. After the 1975 reorganisation, when Midlothian became a district within Lothian Region, Musselburgh and Inveresk were transferred to East Lothian, and Edinburgh became a separate district, effectively separating Midlothian from the coast.[4] On 1st April 1996, Midlothian once again became responsible for its own affairs as a unitary authority, and Dalkeith is the seat of the new Midlothian Council.

Erected as a burgh of barony for James Douglas of Dalkeith, later first earl of Morton, at the turn of the fifteenth century, Dalkeith passed to the Buccleuchs in the mid seventeenth century.[5] Strategically located at the centre of the Lothian coalfields and the rich agricultural hinterland, the town soon prospered. The Dalkeith to Edinburgh Railway opened in 1831,[6] by which time the town was rivalling Haddington as the largest grain-market in Scotland.[7] The A68 trunk road, which runs through the centre of the town, has ensured its prosperity as well as its congestion.[8]

the geology and natural resources of Midlothian

South-east Scotland, like the rest of northern Britain, has a long and complex geological history, which has resulted in a wide variety of rocks and physical features. Tectonic movements along two major dislocations of the earth's crust, the Southern Uplands Fault and the Highland Boundary Fault, have created three principal structural and physiographic divisions, the Highlands, the Midland Valley and the Southern Uplands.[9] Dalkeith lies in the central division, the Midland Valley.

The Midland Valley has, in effect, dropped down between two great faults, the Highland Boundary Fault to the north, from Stonehaven to the Firth of Clyde at Helensburgh, and the Southern Upland Fault to the south, from Dunbar through New Cumnock to Glen App. Here, Old Red Sandstone and Carboniferous rocks are preserved within a trough 50 miles wide, resulting in a broad lowland tract of good farming and industrial development. Old Red Sandstone in the north passes eastwards beneath the rich soils of Strathmore, and is separated by the hard igneous and volcanic rocks of the Sidlaw and Ochil Hills and Campsie Fells from the industrial south. Here, fairly intensive farming surrounds and serves the four-fifths of the population of Scotland which has concentrated around the coal-bearing rocks and oil-shales and their attendant heavy industry. Within this undulating lowland landscape, there are sharp irregularities of igneous rock, forming conspicuous landmarks: for example, North Berwick Law and Traprain Law, near Haddington, in East Lothian; the dolerite hills of Fife; the Castle Rock of Stirling; and volcanics of the Bathgate Hills and Arthur's Seat.[10] These peaks also provide a useful reminder that the term Midland 'Valley' is somewhat misleading as much of the land lies above 120 metres OD.[11]

Sedimentary rocks, such as Old Red Sandstone, are generally softer than igneous rocks, so they tend not to form prominent features of the landscape. During the Carboniferous period (285–350 million years ago), when most of the rocks underlying Edinburgh and most of central Scotland were formed, the Old Red Sandstone mountains (formed during the Devonian period 350–400 million years ago) were worn down to plains with shallow lagoons and seas. This period was also characterised by rapidly changing environments, some long-lived, others short-lived, which resulted in the deposition of alternating layers of rock and strata. For example, luxuriant forest growth, developed during humid, equatorial conditions, ultimately formed the thick coal seams known as the Limestone Coal Formation and the Coal Measures. Tropical seas encouraged limestones with corals, shells and other fossil remains in the Lower Limestone Formation. Lagoons with organic-rich mud also developed giving rise to the oil-shales of West Lothian.[12] These seams of coal, ironstones, limestones and oil-shales formed the basis of the industrialisation of the Midland Valley during the nineteenth and first part of the twentieth centuries, and were extensively exploited.[13] Midlothian has some of the richest coal reserves in the country with up to thirty-four workable seams in places, measuring some thirty metres in thickness.[14] The more recently opened collieries in the Midlothian coalfield, like Bilston Glen and Monktonhall, were designed to exploit the very deep reserves of the Lower Coals. Earlier collieries had mined only the Upper Coals, which had been largely exhausted by the mid twentieth century. The abundant coal reserves of Midlothian also determined the ultimate location of the Scottish salt industry which transformed sea-water into salt.[15] Coal replaced timber and peat in the evaporating process, resulting in a concentration of salt-panning works along the Lothian coastline, with a particular concentration around Prestonpans.

Like coal mining, the lime industry flourished over much of Midlothian, providing lime for the Edinburgh building industry and for local farmers. The landscape is still dotted with disused limekilns which stand like dwarf forts, as at Crichton.[16]

At the end of the Carboniferous period the record of geological strata ends and no further sediments were preserved in the Edinburgh area.[17] From 250 million to two million years ago the area was mainly dry land, the mountains being eroded by weathering and by large rivers which flowed into seas, occupying the North Sea and south-east England.[18]

For much of the last two million years northern Britain has been repeatedly buried under an ice-cap hundreds of metres thick, the latest of which melted as recently as fifteen thousand years ago. During each successive ice age in Scotland, ice built up in the Highlands and Southern Uplands and merged in the Midland Valley before flowing from west to east across the country. The tremendous weight and power of the ice caps eroded the softer sedimentary rock, leaving harder, mainly volcanic rock as hills. Glacial till, commonly known as boulder clay, a mixture of tough clay, ground-down mudstone and siltstone, together with the remains of boulders, sandstones and limestones, was also deposited by the ice.[19]

Warmer spells between the ice ages, the most recent of which began fifteen thousand years ago (ie we are presently in an inter-glacial period), allowed the ice to melt and the ice-cap to recede. This also produced vast amounts of melt-water which cut new valleys and gorges, and transported glacial debris. The coarser materials were deposited as mounds and terraces of sand and gravels as in the Esk valley, which, like the coal reserves, have been extensively exploited. The lighter materials, such as silts and clays, were carried on to be deposited in lochs and in the sea.[20]

soils, agriculture and climate

The preservation of oak woods at Roslin Glen and Dalkeith House gives an impression of the ancient landscape prior to the 'improvements' of the eighteenth century and the industrialisation of Midlothian.[21] Only at the foot of the Lammermuir Hills are there remnants of the old agricultural landscape. Here, open fields, twisting roads and scattered villages are all that remain of the settlements that once covered the poorer, more acid soils of the upland fringe.[22]

The climate is warm and moderately dry with rainfall in the range of 600–850 mm per annum. A wide range of crops can be grown, but the land may be unsuited to the more difficult winter-harvested crops. High yields of cereals and grass can be achieved together with moderate yields of potatoes, some vegetable crops and oil seed rape.[23] Over recent years farming in Midlothian has changed significantly, with dairy farming replaced by intensive cash cropping. Sheep farming, however, continues on the southern uplands, despite the steady encroachment of forestry.

physical setting and topography of the burgh **figures 2 & 3**

The historic (medieval) core of Dalkeith occupies a narrow ridge between the two branches of the River Esk, a distance of some 550 m. The High Street follows the ridge top (approximately 60 m OD) on a north-east to south-west alignment. Even as late as John Lesslie's *Plan of Dalkeith c* 1770 **figure 11**, the town comprised little more than a High Street development. A combination of natural and man-made features framed the development of the town. The grounds of Dalkeith House provided a limit to the eastern expansion of the burgh, with the two rivers forming natural boundaries to the north and south. The Old Edinburgh Road probably formed the western boundary.

Lesslie's *c* 1770 map, however, does offer a convenient starting point for defining the medieval core of the town and its subsequent development. The church of St Nicholas occupies a central position on the north side of the High Street and stands within its own churchyard. On this same side of the street, to the east of the church, the properties that front onto the street may have had no formal burgage plots, with what appears to have been open land extending north to the bank of the River North Esk. On the opposite side of the street the burgage plots are well defined, extending southwards to a back lane (now St Andrew Street). Between the lane and the bank of the River South Esk lay an area of enclosed fields of varying size.

An examination of the burgage plots suggests, at first glance, that the northern end of the town was the most dynamic part of the townscape. The subdivision of the plots here might be seen as an indication of the development pressures and commercial activity normally associated with a market place. This is not the case, however: it is largely the result of nineteenth-century expansion and traffic management measures. The medieval market place always seems to have been in front of the old parish church of St Nicholas.

Some development had also been attracted along the road between the two main river crossings, from Bridgend to Newmills (now the Old Edinburgh Road and Buccleuch Street). To the north of the town along the south bank of the River North Esk were a number of mills. A lade, which drew water from the river, powered an oat mill, flour mill, a barley mill and waulk mill, all clearly visible on Lesslie's map **figure 11**.

notes

1 J Thomas, *Midlothian: An Illustrated Architectural Guide* (Edinburgh, 1995), 3.
2 *Ibid*, 3.
3 J Keay & J Keay (edd), *Collins Encyclopaedia of Scotland* (London, 1994), 695.
4 Thomas, *Midlothian*, 3.
5 G S Pryde, *The Burghs of Scotland: A Critical List* (London, 1965), 48.
6 C McWilliam (ed), *The Buildings of Scotland: Lothian except Edinburgh* (Edinburgh, 1978), 162.

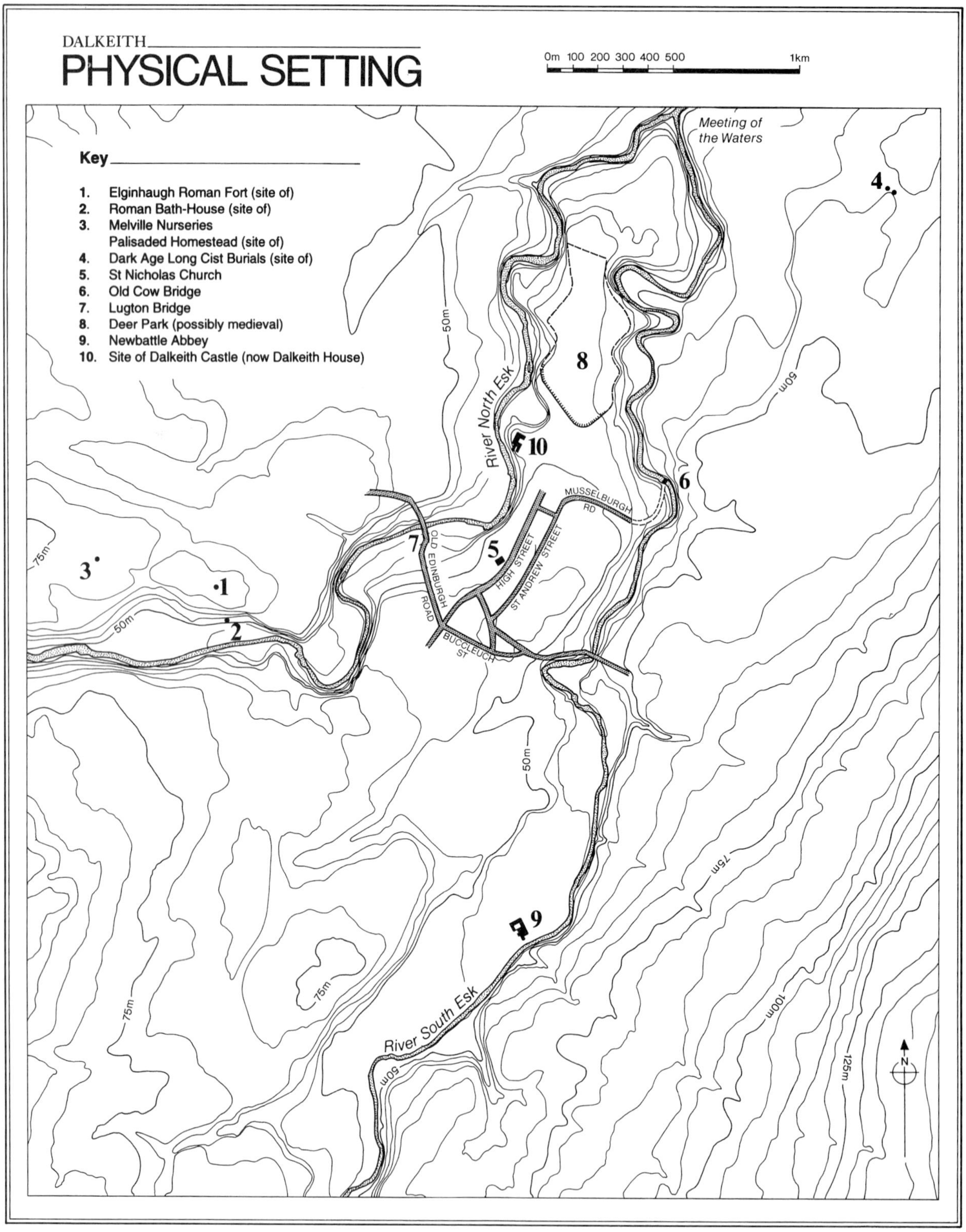

figure 2

The physical setting of Dalkeith

7 *OSA*, 212.

8 Keay & Keay, *Scotland*, 214.

9 C J Brown & B M Shipley, *Soil Survey of Scotland: South East Scotland. Soil and Land Capability for Agriculture* (The Macaulay Institute for Soil Research, Aberdeen, 1982), 2. The three major land divisions (Highlands, Midland Valley and Southern Uplands) follow J B Sissons, *The Geomorphology of the British Isles: Scotland* (London, 1976).

10 E Edmonds, *The Geological Map. An Anatomy of the Landscape* (London, 1983), 18.

11 J Whittow, *Geology and Scenery in Britain* (London, 1992), 265.

12 D McAdam, *Edinburgh: A Landscape Fashioned by Geology* (British Geological Survey for Scottish Natural Heritage, Battleby, 1993), 10.

13 I B Cameron & D Stephenson, *The*

figure 3
Dalkeith from the air
1948

Midland Valley of Scotland (British Regional Geology, 3rd edn, London, 1985), 6.
14 Keay & Keay, *Scotland*, 174.
15 Whittow, *Geology*, 288.
16 Thomas, *Midlothian*, 5.
17 McAdam, *Edinburgh*, 11.
18 *Ibid*, 16.
19 *Ibid*, 12.
20 *Ibid*, 12.
21 Whittow, *Geology*, 287.
22 *Ibid*, 287.
23 Brown & Shipley, *Soil Survey*, Sheet 7.

archaeological and historical background

pp 11–46

D

archaeological and historical background

A large number of prehistoric and, particularly, Roman sites and finds are known from around Dalkeith, although to date no archaeological work has been undertaken within the historic (medieval) core of the burgh. An introduction to the prehistory of the area is included here, in order to place these ancient sites and finds in context and to provide a broader framework within which to study the origins of the medieval burgh. This includes an extended section on the Roman period and the fort at Elginhaugh, which lies close to Dalkeith **figure 2**, to place occupation here within the overall pattern of Roman Scotland.

prehistory

The earliest settlement of Scotland occurred around 7,000 BC, when much of the country was covered in dense woodland which supported a rich variety of game, particularly red deer. The few Mesolithic (literally meaning Middle Stone Age) settlements known in Scotland tend to be found along the coast line and river banks. These communities were 'hunter-gatherers' who ate fish and shellfish, followed herds of woodland game through the seasons, and supplemented their diet with wild plants and berries. Their semi-nomadic existence has left few archaeological traces, although shell middens and flint tools are common finds along former river and coast lines. Numerous Mesolithic flints were recovered from beneath the rampart of the Roman fort at Elginhaugh (*see below*).

Around 3,500 BC, people began to live a more settled existence in response to changes in the environment, including more favourable soil conditions, and to ideas introduced from continental Europe. Large areas of woodland were cleared by burning and trees were cut down with stone tools, livestock was kept and the land farmed for crops. A polished flint adze found in 1967 at Smeatons Bridge (now in the National Museums of Scotland) is an example of the kind of tool used in clearing the land; fragments of late Neolithic pottery have also been found locally, at the Woodburn Housing Estate. Again, few traces of these Neolithic (literally meaning New Stone Age) settlements survive, but the landscape still bears testament to the presence of these people, in the form of ritual enclosures (including henges) and burial mounds.

Ritual is strongly evidenced in the lives of these early farming groups, particularly in their treatment of the dead, who were buried in monumental tombs. These communal stone-built chambered cairns or barrows constructed of wood and turf sometimes contained large numbers of burials. There is considerable regional variation in the types and styles of these monuments, no doubt reflecting local traditions and perhaps the origins of the societies which used them.[1] The tombs probably became a focus for ritual where elaborate ceremonies took place, perhaps in celebration of ancestors.

By about 2,500 BC, changes in society were gradually taking place and monuments such as stone circles were erected, apparently incorporating an awareness of the rising and setting of the sun and moon in their design.[2] The tradition of monumental tombs containing large numbers of burials waned in favour of a new trend for single grave burials. Bronze Age people also developed new styles of pottery, unenclosed settlements and metal-working. Close to Dalkeith, excavations at the Roman fort of Elginhaugh (*see below* pp 14–16) also produced evidence of much earlier peoples. Sealed well beneath a Roman road was a shallow pit containing different types of Bronze Age Beakers; while, on the east side of the fort, a number of shallow pits contained traces of burning and late Bronze Age or early Iron Age pottery.

A number of Bronze Age burials have been found in and around Dalkeith, representing two different traditions of burial: inhumation and cremation. Both traditions usually contain the body, or an urn containing cremated remains, within a small stone-lined cist set beneath a stone cairn, although some cremation urns were placed in a pit. Very often the cairn has since been robbed away, leaving only the cist. Some were single, isolated burials but others were part of larger cemeteries; cairns were often reused and can contain a number of later burials inserted into the flanks or top of the mound. These burials often contained personal possessions, perhaps for use in the afterlife; these possessions could reflect the position of the deceased individual within the overall social hierarchy. Other finds of this period have also been found in and around Dalkeith. In a barrow (or mound) discovered at Newbattle Abbey, surrounded by a stone circle, was a stone cist containing a male skeleton. A cinerary urn was found in or near the town in the nineteenth century, and a bronze cauldron was discovered almost 1 m below the ground surface on the Woodburn Housing Estate.

Early Bronze Age occupation was also indicated at the site of Elginhaugh. Sealed well beneath the Roman roadway was a pebble surface adjacent to a shallow pit which contained both All Over Corded and Rusticated Beakers; while beneath the *intervallum* roadway of the fort on the east side were a number of shallow pits containing traces of burning and Late Bronze Age or Early Iron Age pottery.

Considerable changes in technology and in society took place at the end of the Bronze Age, around 600 BC. Iron tools and, increasingly, weapons begin to appear in the archaeological record. Despite the abundance of evidence for monuments and rich burials in the Neolithic and Bronze Age, knowledge of the subsistence base which supported these societies, and the settlements in which they lived, is rather poor.[3] By the late Bronze Age/early Iron Age, however, settlements begin to dominate the archaeological landscape. Numerous fortified settlements, ranging from large hill forts to enclosed villages and isolated single family dwellings, are known. Less defensive types of settlement also existed, but the remains from this period seem generally to reflect a more competitive society, in which groups perhaps fought over natural resources. The impression is that there was a move away from large monuments that served the community in the second and third millennia BC, towards settlements indicative of tribal divisions.[4]

later prehistory

The Iron Age archaeological landscape of the Esk valley and the area around Dalkeith is particularly rich, comprising literally hundreds of pit alignments (prehistoric landscape divisions), ring-ditches, rectangular enclosures and field systems. The increasing use of aerial photography as a survey technique in recent years has led to the identification of very many previously unknown archaeological sites, only visible as cropmarks from the air. These discoveries are gradually filling in the gaps in our knowledge of prehistoric settlement. Large numbers of enclosed and unenclosed settlements have now been identified. Without excavation, cropmarks can be difficult to ascribe to a particular period, but they have greatly increased our awareness of the complexity of settlement patterns. There has been one excavation of such a site in the Dalkeith area. In 1982, housing development provided an opportunity to excavate a pit alignment at Eskbank Nurseries (NT 320 668). The excavation showed that the site consisted of a linear series of pits, which had been dug in the late pre-Roman Iron Age and subsequently infilled by a gradual process of natural weathering. The excavator interpreted the pits as quarry pits which were used to provide material for the bank of a linear earthwork, probably some form of land division.[5] An assessment of how many of the broad range of newly identified settlement types and field systems were contemporary with the Roman occupation of the Lothians and the fort at Elginhaugh, for example, is an important avenue for further research.[6] A programme of work has been underway, though largely dictated by development pressures, and several sites have now been excavated. Close to Dalkeith a native Iron Age settlement was excavated at Melville Nurseries in 1989 **figures 2 & 4**. Here, a double ring of post-holes marked the outline of a timber-built roundhouse with a slightly scooped floor; while nearby, the remains of another probable roundhouse and several cooking pits were contained within a fenced enclosure.[7]

the Roman period

It was this, perhaps more fragmented, Iron Age society which the Romans encountered in the first century AD. According to Ptolemy, the classical geographer, whose map of the Roman world was compiled around AD 140, the Lothians were within the tribal domain

figure 4
The Iron Age palisaded homestead and pit alignments at Melville Nurseries from the air 1992
© Crown Copyright: RCAHMS

of the Votadini. Their capital was probably at Traprain Law, near East Linton (NT 581 746).

The security of the northern frontier was founded on a treaty between Rome and the Brigantian Queen, Cartimandua. Demonstrating how fragile these arrangements could be, during the Civil War of AD 68/9 she was ousted by her husband, the anti-Roman Venutius.[8] A series of campaigns from AD 71 to 74 returned control of the area to Rome; and it is possible that the first Roman penetration into southern Scotland, under the new governor, Q Petillius Cerialis, dates to this time.[9] A new dynasty, beginning with Emperor Vespasian in AD 69, had by now attained power in Rome. A loyal supporter of this newly established Flavian dynasty was one Gnaeus Julius Agricola, with whom the early Roman history of Scotland is inextricably linked. His son-in-law, the distinguished historian Cornelius Tacitus, wrote an account of Agricola's life. Chosen as the new governor in AD 77, Agricola first campaigned in Wales and northern England, before moving into Scotland and advancing without much opposition to the Tay. The following year was spent consolidating and garrisoning the new frontier zone. In particular, he established a line of garrisons in the valley between the Forth and the Clyde;[10] one of these garrisons was presumably Elginhaugh by Dalkeith. In AD 81 he probably campaigned into south-west Scotland, pondering an expedition to Ireland and perhaps considering routes up the west coast.[11] In AD 82 he advanced beyond the Forth. This, his sixth campaign, culminated in the defeat of the Caledonians under Calgacus at the battle of Mons

Graupius, in AD 83. The site of this famous battle possibly lies somewhere in north-east Scotland.[12] This was the climax of Agricola's governorship and he shortly afterwards returned to Rome.

It was left to his unknown successor to consolidate Agricola's advances, with a system of roads and forts established throughout central and eastern Scotland, and extending the length of Strathmore. This included forts strategically placed at the mouths of the Highland glens, but the nerve centre was the 53 acre (21.5 ha) legionary fortress at Inchuthil on the Tay. Whether further military campaigns were intended is uncertain, but Inchtuthil was demolished before construction was even completed.[13] The reason for this dramatic shift in policy was a series of military disasters in the Balkans, with the result that troops had to be redeployed from elsewhere in the Empire. Inchtuthil and all the forts north of a line from Newstead to Glenlochar were abandoned *c* AD 87. By the turn of the century, the Romans had fallen back as far as the Tyne–Solway line, where forts were connected by the road known as the Stanegate.

In the early AD 120s, it was a line slightly further north that the Emperor Hadrian chose for the construction of a massive barrier of turf and stone—Hadrian's Wall. As the northern frontier of the empire, it was short-lived; in AD 138 Hadrian's successor, Antoninus Pius, ordered his army to advance into central Scotland and begin construction of a second great barrier, the Antonine Wall. Built in the years after AD 142, it may have owed more to a need for personal recognition than to any military strategy. The Wall stretched for some 60 km between Bo'ness on the Forth and Old Kilpatrick on the Clyde, with fortlets probably at every mile and forts at wider intervals. New forts were established south of the Wall, many on or close by sites of abandoned forts, with some north of the Wall, up to the Tay. These forts were abandoned in the AD 160s, when the army was withdrawn to the line of Hadrian's Wall. Some forts were retained as outposts, in Dumfriesshire and up to the Tweed, but by about AD 180 most of these were abandoned. Once again Hadrian's Wall became the northern frontier of Roman Britain.

There was one final episode in the history of Roman Scotland. For a variety of reasons, the Emperor Septimius Severus, together with his sons Caracalla and Geta, arrived in Britain in AD 208 to mount a major campaign in the north, specifically against two tribes—the Maeatae, whose territory seems to have been Stirlingshire, Strathearn and Strathmore, and the Caledonians who were based further north.[14] Probably accompanied by a fleet, Severus and his army advanced beyond Hadrian's Wall, through eastern Scotland and up the east coast. Despite taking the title *Britannicus*, 'conqueror of Britain', Severus' celebrations were short-lived, for a major rebellion occurred in the following year. Construction work on a new fortress at Carpow, on the Tay near Newburgh, suggests that the Romans intended to stay. Severus died in AD 211. His son Caracalla succeeded him and immediately returned to Rome, abandoning the Scottish conquests.[15] Hadrian's Wall was again reinstated as the northern frontier of the province, with some forts garrisoned in the Cheviots as out-posts. By the late third century AD the Picts—probably a new power grouping amongst the tribes—and others were putting increasing pressure on the northern frontier. Hadrian's Wall appears to have been garrisoned until the early years of the fifth century AD, before Britain was finally abandoned by Rome.

Roman Elginhaugh

The auxiliary fort and annexe at Elginhaugh (NT 321 673 **figure 2**) probably dates from Agricola's fourth campaign in the first century AD.[16] The siting of a fort here owes much to the strategic requirements of the occupying army;[17] Elginhaugh lies at the junction of the two principal north–south routes through Scotland. Dere Street connected Corbridge on the Tyne with the forts on the Forth–Clyde isthmus, passing through Newstead, near Melrose; this route followed the line of the modern A68 trunk road. The second route was more circuitous, running north from Carlisle, through Annandale and upper Clydesdale, and then cutting obliquely across country through the Biggar Gap and

figure 5
The Roman fort at Elginhaugh during excavation 1986
© Crown Copyright RCAHMS

along the south-east Pentland Hills. It joined up with Dere Street at Elginhaugh, the main bridgehead over the North Esk. The road running west from the fort itself towards the line of the modern A7 is thought to be the course followed by Dere Street running north-west to Liberton. The North Esk must have been crossed in the vicinity of the fort; the crossing point on the South Esk is not known.

In 1980, a section was cut through the foundation of a Roman road of the late first century AD by Elginhaugh. The foundation, a levelled surface of sand, pebbles and gravel about 9.5 m wide, was lined on each side by a ditch about 1.5 m wide and 0.3 m deep. The ditch fills contained pottery, including a small fragment of a samian dish of southern Gaulish manufacture. Agricultural operations over the centuries have removed the upper layers of road metalling.

The Elginhaugh fort itself (NT 321 673), set on the crest of a steep scarp by the North Esk, some 250 m north of Elginhaugh Bridge, was identified by aerial photography in 1979, with an annexe identified on the north-west side of the fort and a bathhouse at the foot of the scarp to the south. The fort was completely excavated in 1986 **figure 5** and proved to be late first century in date. Within a turf rampart 6–8 m wide and defended by three or four ditches, the fort covered a total area of 1.26 ha. Towers flanked each of the four gateways and there were also towers at the corners and at intermediate positions in the rampart. Inside the fort, the central range comprised the headquarters building, the commanding officer's house and two granaries, and there were barrack-blocks and storage buildings to both front and rear. All but one of the buildings in the interior were of timber. A stone building set against the back of the rampart at the north-east corner may have been a workshop; several stone-built ovens were also set against the rampart and a system of stone-built drains lined the roads. A large assemblage of finds included pottery, glass, a steelyard, a bronze *patera*, a bronze key, an iron shield boss, a cache of unused nails and a hoard of forty-one *denarii*, the latest dating to AD 77–8. The latest coin from the fort as a whole was minted in AD 86.

In 1987, parts of the fort annexe were also excavated and occupation was found to be concentrated alongside the road which ran through the annexe from the west gate of the fort. Three phases of re-surfacing indicated that traffic had been quite heavy. The earliest activity involved a number of ovens or furnaces, probably associated with grain processing, which were later replaced by timber buildings fronting onto the road. Later still, the roadside area seems again to have been given over to cooking ovens, before being cut off from the rest of the annexe by two ditches. These ditches served perhaps to 'funnel' the movement of animals from the outer ditches of the fort to the annexe gateway.

A bathhouse, located south of the fort (NT 321 672), measured *c* 23 by 7.5 m and trial trenches have confirmed that its walling stands eleven courses high in places.

In addition to the Elginhaugh complex, two Roman marching camps have been investigated at nearby Eskbank (NT 321 668). An excavation in 1972 examined the relative chronology of the two superimposed camps and the entrance complex of one of them. One camp was shown to be earlier than the other, but no material which could provide absolute dates was recovered. The entrance of camp A was shown to be 11 m wide and was fronted by a *titulum*, the irregularly-shaped ditch of which was 10.6 m long and less than 1 m deep. No trace of the rampart bank of either camp remained.[18]

Tacitus' account implies that the Forth–Clyde isthmus was a terminus, or frontier. As a result, much attention has been focused on a possible chain of forts here, the *praesidia* referred to by Tacitus. Several forts fit the criteria, of which Elginhaugh is one, with a possible 6–8 mile (9.7–12.9 km) mean spacing between them.[19] The withdrawal from north of the Forth–Clyde isthmus is securely dated to late AD 86 to early AD 88, but the geographical extent of the withdrawal is less certain.[20] Many first-century forts were reoccupied during the Antonine period but Elginhaugh was not, and Roman interest in Dalkeith came to an end. The Elginhaugh excavations identified only one phase of occupation before the fort was deliberately demolished, at a time when lowland Scotland seems to have undergone major rationalisation and reorganisation.[21] Further south, for example, Newstead, a key site in the new strategy, was enlarged by demolishing the existing fort, and rebuilding a larger one.[22]

the early historic period

Major changes occurred in the political organisation of Scotland in the period after the withdrawal of the Romans. By the third century AD, the numerous small tribal groups recorded in Ptolemy's *Geography* seem to have been coalescing into larger confederacies; and, by the fourth century, these confederacies seem themselves to have merged into an even larger grouping known as the Picts. By around the middle of the first millennium AD, the Pictish kingdom dominated Scotland north of the Forth and Clyde estuaries. The exception was Argyll which was occupied by the Dàl Riata Gaels, originally from north-east Ireland, whose name *Gaedil* became translated into Latin as *Scoti*. Eventually, of course, the *Scoti* came to dominate and gave their name to Scotland—but not until the mid ninth century AD, when Kenneth mac Alpin (*c* 843–58) established royal, political and cultural supremacy over the Pictish kingdom.

The four tribes south of the Forth, listed by Ptolemy, seem to have undergone rather less transformation. One of the most important of the Iron Age tribes was the Votadini, centred in Lothian, whose tribal capital was probably on Traprain Law. A few centuries later, Edinburgh's Castle Rock emerges as the fortified capital of the kingdom of the Gododdin—the post-Roman descendants of the Votadini. Their neighbours to the west, the Britons in the kingdom of Strathclyde, seem likewise to have emerged from the Iron Age Damnonii; the Britonnic capital lay on the north side of the Clyde, on Dumbarton Rock. This apparent continuity of peoples in southern Scotland—from the Iron Age, through the Roman period and into the early historic period—was broken only by the arrival of the Angles. The turbulent events of seventh-century Lothian are documented in the epic poem, *y Gododdin*, with its tales of pre-battle feasting at *Din Eidyn* (Edinburgh); and in the *Annals of Ulster* which refers to the '*obsessio Etin*', or siege of Edinburgh, interpreted as an assault on Edinburgh by the Northumbrian Angles under Oswald. This may have been the culmination of a process of annexation, or no more than a daring raid, but it seems that the Anglian kings of Northumbria were in control of much of south-east Scotland, including Lothian, from about the later seventh century AD. After this, the area became 'border land' between the Anglo-Saxons and the Picts; and it was not until the early eleventh century AD that the by-then Scottish kings also gained control of Northumbrian Lothian and Strathclyde.

This period also saw the introduction of Christianity to Scotland. From his base at Whithorn, Wigtownshire, St Ninian is reputed to have led the first Christian mission to southern Pictland in the early fifth century AD. The process was given new impetus by St Columba in the later sixth century from his base at Iona, and the conversion of Pictland and Northumbria was completed probably before the end of the seventh century AD. In the Lothians the teachings of the Northumbrian church spread through the valleys that ran north and south to the Forth, a natural feature which provided an immediate barrier to their aspirations,[23] although Northumbrian Christianity allegedly reached Stirling by the fifth or sixth century (here, by AD 540, a legend had already grown up of Ninian having consecrated a cemetery in the area now known as St Ninians).[24]

In south-east Scotland, Norse, Gaelic, Cumbric or British, Anglian and Pictish place-names are all present for the early historic period. Many denote actual settlement but others are descriptive of geographical features, such as hills, moors and valleys.[25] As might be expected, there is scant evidence for the Norse or Scots, slightly more for the Picts and considerably more for Britons and Angles.[26]

Although the Northumbrian Angles came to dominate south-east Scotland after the seventh century, few of their settlements have been identified. The only three primary late seventh- to eighth-century Anglian names in Scotland—Coldingham, Whittinghame and Tyninghame—all cluster along the narrow, eastern coastal strip, which is also where their early settlement sites are found.[27] At Doon Hill (NT 686755), near Dunbar, a seventh-century timber hall was discovered to overlie the ruins of a sixth-century British hall. Similar sequences have been identified at Yeavering, Northumberland, and two seventh-century timber halls were recently discovered during excavations at Dunbar; while at Ratho, near Edinburgh, a palisade alignment enclosed a sunken-featured building of sixth- or early seventh-century date, which may have been used for weaving and the dyeing of yarn or fabric, and two rectilinear post-in-trench structures were also found.[28] Place-names catalogue the subsequent waves of colonisation: for example, names ending in -ington (farm), -botl (dwelling or dwelling place) and -wic (dependent farm) (*eg* Haddington, Newbattle and Borthwick) are all evidence of later settlement.[29]

No settlements of this later period have been found in the close vicinity of Dalkeith, but other evidence exists in the form of burials and carved stones. Carved stones were found in 1866 at nearby Lasswade, built into the walls of the now-ruined parish church. A cemetery of over fifty long cists (the typical early Christian burial tradition) was discovered in 1938 by labourers digging for sand at Newton (NT 348 688); and two more cists were disturbed in 1970. Other long cists were found at Melville Grange (NT 30 67) in 1864, and there is a tradition of others being found nearby at Parkburn.[30]

the middle ages

There are a number of suggestions as to the origin of the place-name, Dalkeith. It may be of Celtic provenance, meaning 'narrow or contracted vale', which would be an allusion to its distinctive geographical setting between the Rivers North Esk and South Esk; others maintain that it is a Gaelic place-name, 'Dailchata', meaning 'field of battle'.[31] There may, however, be evidence of a lingering Cumbric term—'ced' [wood]—in [Dal]keith.[32]

The first mention of Dalkeith occurs *c* 1143. Some time around this date, David I (1124–53) granted various lands by charter to Holyrood Abbey, including the 'land of Dolchet [Dalkeith] between the woods and the open land in the estate of Ruchale [which had been given to the monks of nearby Newbattle]'. The Cistercian abbey at Newbattle, located by the South Esk and less than 2 km south of Dalkeith **figure 2**, had been founded in 1140 and became one of the wealthiest of the medieval abbeys in Lothian.[33]

The lands of Dalkeith were referred to, again, in a charter of Alwin, abbot of Holyrood, who was abbot prior to 1150.[34] The abbey of Holyrood had received its charter of foundation in 1128, also from David I. One of the witnesses to this charter was William de Graham, and it is known that in the twelfth century the Graham family held Dalkeith.[35] If they held a fortified residence here by this time, it probably suggests that there was also a settlement at Dalkeith.[36] Not only would a castle offer a measure of protection to those who clustered near its gate, but also the occupants of the castle would require the services of more menial persons and a local food supply would be a necessity. Both of these factors would have attracted nearby settlement. This probably means that this early settlement was sited somewhere in the present Dalkeith Parks. No information survives on the form of this early castle but it may well have been of motte and bailey type. Although protected to the north by the rocky fall to the River North Esk, the site would have had little natural protection to the south. The great depth of garden soil discovered to the frontage of the presumed site of this early fortified dwelling may, possibly, be the remnant of an artificial motte **figure 23**. If the early structure was of the motte and bailey type, it was probably replaced by a simple curtain-wall castle (*see* p 21) **figure 6**. There was also a tradition, in the nineteenth century, that the lawns which now stand in front of Dalkeith Palace were formed only after infilling of a river course that ran in front of the palace.[37] This may be evidence of a moat.

Little is known of this early settlement. The barony of Dalkeith was noted by Edward I of England (1272–1307) in 1304, when instructions were given to the sheriff of Edinburgh that Sir Nicholas de Graham should receive sasine of all his due inheritance.[38] It was, apparently, held by one Peter Lubaud for a period of time before March 1316, when it was granted to Robert de Lawder,[39] after which it reverted to the Graham family. Dalkeith was visited by the chronicler Jean Froissart around the year 1361. According to his *Chronicles*, Edward III of England (1327–77) seized the castle of Dalkeith during one of his campaigns, perhaps around 1339, and appointed his own governor and garrison.[40] By the time of Froissart's visit, the castle had passed to the house of Douglas, as a result of the marriage of Marjory de Graham to William Douglas of Lugton in the middle of the fourteenth century.[41] The latter was to be succeeded by his nephew, James, second earl of Douglas, who was created first lord of Dalkeith in 1369 by David II (1329–71), receiving for himself and his heirs the barony and castle of Dalkeith 'on giving annually to the king at the castle of Dalkeith, if sought, a pair of white gloves or a silver penny at the feast of Pentecost'. He was also granted the right to free forest at Dalkeith, which gave him rights over previously royal forest.[42] In 1370, the castle was undergoing repair work and/or extension.[43] The first lord of Dalkeith was to die at the battle of Otterburn, in 1388.[44]

References to Dalkeith in the fourteenth century may be not to the settlement, but rather to the barony or the castle. In 1351, for example, a charter was signed at Dalkeith, but this was probably effected in the castle.[45] That the castle itself was undergoing repairs or reconstruction in 1369/1370 would imply the presence of a local workforce.[46] In the

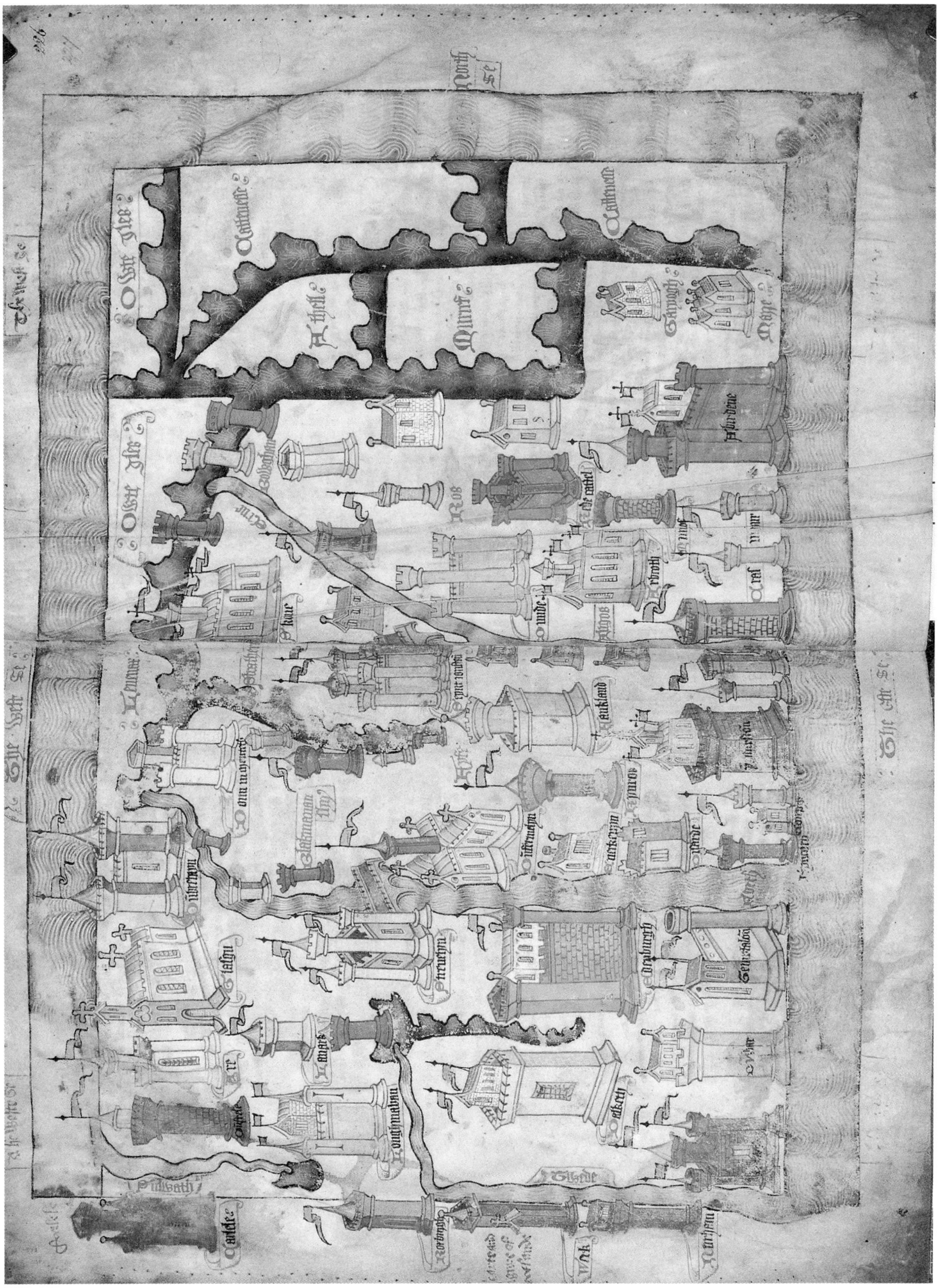

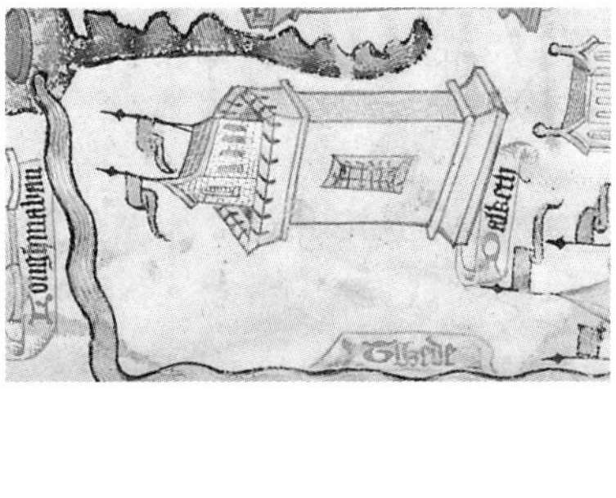

figure 6
John Harding's map of Scottish castles 1457
Detail of Dalkeith Castle *above*

figure 7
The fifteenth-century tomb of James Douglas, first earl of Morton, and his wife Joanna

same year a chantry was founded in the chapel of Dalkeith,[47] but whether this means that a chapel stood in the little township or was established within the castle is unclear. A chapel was certainly founded in the township in the later fourteenth century, although its exact date of foundation is less sure. Some believe, perhaps correctly, that as early as 1372 consent was given to found a chaplainry in the chapel of St Nicholas, which stood in the town.[48] In 1377, a grant of land in Peebles was made to the chapel, but whether this referred to a chapel in the castle or the township is not stated.[49] It is to be expected that the castle had a chapel, and it has been argued, elsewhere, that this was so;[50] that chaplainries dedicated to the Virgin Mary and John the Baptist had been established in it by 1377 (although there may be here an element of confusion with St Nicholas Chapel);[51] and that a further chaplainry was endowed in the castle in 1384.[52] It is quite possible, however, that there was a chapel in both the castle and the town. Certainly, by 1386, or possibly 1396, the chapel of St Nicholas had been erected in the town. In June of that year, a hospital for six poor people was founded beside the chapel by Sir James Douglas.[53] Although there is an element of disagreement about whether this hospital was founded in 1386 or 1396 (thus determining a date for latest foundation of the town chapel, since the hospital stood beside it), the fact that the chapel of St Nicholas was undergoing repairs to its roof in 1390, at a cost of £20, is firm indication of its existence by this date, and perhaps as early as 1372 (*see above*).[54]

In 1405, a provost and five chaplains were endowed by Sir James on the chapel of St Nicholas, thus raising it to the status of a collegiate church. It may have undergone some rebuilding around 1420.[55] It is known that one of the altars was dedicated to the Blessed Virgin, as a charter was signed at it in 1432.[56] This may have stood in the choir of the church.[57] By 1467 the collegiate church was to become, also, the parish church of Dalkeith, as opposed to being subordinate to the parish church of Lasswade.[58] In 1475 and 1477, the college was expanded by James Douglas, the first earl of Morton, whose tomb, along with that of his wife, Joanna, daughter of King James I (1406–37), lies in the choir **figure 7**; and in 1503 two further chaplainries were established, dedicated to the Holy Rood and St John the Baptist.[59] The altar dedicated to St John the Baptist stood in the south aisle.[60] References in 1504 and 1557 to a chaplainry dedicated to the Crucifix may be indication of a new endowment, although this may simply be the chaplainry of the Holy Rood under another name.[61] There were also, apparently, two further altars, that dedicated to St Peter, which stood in the north transept, and that dedicated to St Nicholas, which was in the centre of the chancel.[62]

It is clear that by as early as the end of the fourteenth century, the small settlement had grown sufficiently to be referred to as a 'villa' or town, although, in reality, it would have been little more than a village in size.[63] In 1401 Robert III (1390–1406) granted to Sir James Douglas, first lord of Dalkeith, that his 'villa' should be held as a free burgh of barony.[64] (In 1540, it was elevated to the status of a burgh of regality.)[65] Presumably having the right to hold a market, one of the basic rights of burghs, the town would have attracted traders from the surrounding rural hinterland. Increased trade meant increased prosperity, not only for the burgh superior, but for the town itself as well. The records make it clear, however, that the atmosphere was essentially rural.[66] Although there is little evidence, it is fair to assume that the townscape was expanding in the fifteenth century. By 1430, and probably of very much earlier date, the main street, called 'the great road', was established and lined with burgage plots.[67] An interesting depiction of Dalkeith Castle has survived. Although stylised, and probably not correct in detail, it portrays a tower within a simple enclosure wall, which was probably correct for this period **figure 6**.

In 1452, the town and castle were in the possession of James Douglas, third lord of Dalkeith. They were plundered and burned by his kinsman, James, ninth earl of Douglas,[68] who had renounced his allegiance to King James II (1437–60). This was in retaliation for the murder of William, the eighth earl, by the king.[69] The burning of Dalkeith was one of a number of crimes for which the ninth earl was subsequently forfeited in 1455.[70] This attack may have led to increased hardship for the small township, and 1452 was a year of general dearth.[71] Dalkeith was accustomed to various military manoeuvres, given its strategic location on the main route between Edinburgh and the border. In 1497, for example, the cannon known as Mons Meg and other artillery were present in the town, on their return journey to Edinburgh following an expedition to the Borders in support of the claim of Perkin Warbeck to the English throne.[72]

the sixteenth century

The relationships of the lords of Dalkeith with the crown brought increased status for the Douglas family. It is known that James II had been resident in Dalkeith in 1444;[73] and that the fourth lord of Dalkeith, James Douglas, was created Earl of Morton in 1457. The second earl, John Douglas, was one of the nobles who met Princess Margaret, eldest daughter of Henry VII of England (1485–1509), in 1503 at Lamberton Kirk in the Borders and escorted her to Newbattle Abbey, on her route to meet her husband, King James IV (1488–1513). It was at Dalkeith Castle that King James met his future bride.[74] The couple remained there for four days, the king returning daily from Edinburgh and affairs of state.[75] A serious fire took hold at this time, probably in the stables of the castle as the new queen's horses were killed and all their bridles and gear destroyed. A pavilion also was lost in the flames; and cloth of gold to the cost of £122 10s Scots was provided to replace it.[76] She still had sufficient possessions for twenty-two carts to be needed to transport them to Edinburgh; each carter was paid six shillings for his trouble.[77] Dalkeith Castle was considered a worthy place for King James V (1513–42) and his court to reside in, when fear of plague forced them out of Edinburgh in September 1519.[78] The arrival of the entire royal court must have had a tremendous impact on the town, particularly as severe restrictions were placed on the townspeople and some houses shut up, for fear of any harm coming to the king.[79]

Dalkeith Castle was often the resting place for royalty during the sixteenth century; and the townspeople must have found the royal retinue and noblemen a common sight. Meetings of the privy council were held in the town on a number of occasions: at least twenty between 1569 and 1578, twenty-three or more between 1578 and 1585, at least thirteen in the seven years from 1585 and 1592, and eighteen or more between 1592 and 1604.[80] In April 1601, James VI (1567–1625) decided that the council called for the 30th

figure 8
John Slezer's view of Dalkeith Castle (mistitled *Glamms House*), *c* 1690

of the month in Linlithgow should, instead, meet in Dalkeith. His main, stated, reason for this was that many of those called to the council lived nearby and residents of Edinburgh could travel home for the night.[81] There must, however, have been many occasions over the previous century when the people of Dalkeith were called upon to provide board and lodgings.

In 1525, in the following year at Christmas, and in 1536 it is known that James V (1513–42) was in residence.[82] Mary, Queen of Scots (1542–67) spent a few days there in October/November 1565.[83] The fourth earl, James Douglas, took a central stage in Scottish politics (for a while as Regent Morton), until his execution in 1581; but not before rebuilding the castle and converting it into a 'magnificent palace' called, contemporaneously, the 'Lion's Den',[84] where he entertained the young James VI 'with great honour' in 1579.[85] The precise design of this palace is uncertain, although remnants of it form part of the present Dalkeith House (*see* pp 74–5). It is known that, as well as being a sumptuous residence, it also had a castle yard, as it was here, under the ground, that Morton allegedly hid his treasure. The depiction of Dalkeith Palace by Slezer over a hundred years later probably reveals a strong likeness to the palace as it was in Morton's time, showing as it does the remnants of an earlier tower structure in the corner **figure 8**.[86] Within nine days of Morton's death, James VI entered the palace, from the parish church of St Nicholas, with two pipers leading his procession.[87] Morton's lands, including Dalkeith, were forfeit to the crown and bestowed on Esmé Stewart, later Duke of Lennox. He resided, for a while, in Dalkeith Castle, before his departure and death in France in 1583.[88] The following year, the attainder was reversed and the lands of Dalkeith reverted back to the house of Douglas.[89]

In 1589, it was claimed that the king would borrow Dalkeith for his new queen, Anna of Denmark, to stay in, as it was 'the nighest fair house to Edinburgh'.[90] The palace was considered of sufficient sumptuousness that it was mooted that it would be one of the places James VI would take his queen in March 1591. The local people were, therefore, instructed to supply 'meit, drink and ludgeing at their reasonable expenses'.[91] He was certainly in residence there in March 1592, when Edinburgh was instructed to furnish him with twenty soldiers for a month to wait on him at Dalkeith,[92] and on 9 August 1592,[93] and it was in the palace that his wife gave birth to a daughter on Christmas Eve, 1598. On this occasion the revelry at the court offended a number of Protestant ministers.[94] It was said, by a visitor to Dalkeith a century later, that Queen Anna kept her court there during the absences of the king.[95] This may be correct; but a contemporary account, in 1592, noted that the queen was to retire to Dalkeith 'where she likes not to abide'.[96]

Visitations were not always splendid affairs. The town continued, throughout the century, to witness a variety of military activities. There was a cannon, for example, in Dalkeith in 1513, en route to the border for the campaign which concluded with the disastrous defeat at the Battle of Flodden. The cannon ran over an ox and broke its neck, and the animal had to be replaced at a cost of thirty-two shillings. The local workmen, however, were given the unfortunate ox to eat.[97] For a while in 1542, Cardinal David Beaton was warded in Dalkeith Castle, for his opposition to the proposed marriage of the young Queen Mary with Prince Edward, the son of Henry VIII of England (1509–47).[98] The choice of Dalkeith was determined by the fact that it was 'a very strong house'.[99] James Douglas, third earl of Morton, espoused the English cause, as a consequence of which Dalkeith Castle was besieged and taken by the governor, James, second earl of Arran, in 1543. Expenses are detailed in the *Treasurer's Accounts* not merely for the siege of the castle, but also for its provisioning thereafter.[100] Newbattle Abbey suffered similar ordeals; it was destroyed *c* 1545 by Edward Seymour, earl of Hertford (later duke of Somerset).

A few years later, in 1547, the town was once again to witness the devastation of war, when hundreds of fugitives fled to Dalkeith after the disastrous defeat of the Scots at the Battle of Pinkie (by Musselburgh); and in the same year the garrison at Dalkeith Castle, under Sir George Douglas, fell to an English siege. In 1548, the town was burned by the English,[101] and 'the house of Dalkeith was destroyed'.[102] On 8 June 1550, it was reported that Dalkeith, along with other towns, was subject to 'birning, utir hirschip and distructioun' by the English, which is probably a reference to the 1548 attack.[103] On 28 June, Captain William Stewart was posted with 500 men 'for resistance to the English'.[104] The town was also to be used as the base, in 1560, for the Protestant Lords of the Congregation, when in opposition to the Roman Catholic regent, Mary of Guise.[105] During the subsequent civil war, following the deposition of her daughter, Queen Mary, in 1567, Dalkeith suffered considerable disruption, not least because the Earl of Morton was a leading figure in the king's party, supporting the young King James VI. During this period, the town ordnance and artillery were stored in the church;[106] and in February 1572, Dalkeith was twice burned by a group of attackers,[107] destroying many houses[108] and all the corn of Morton, who would become regent in 1572.[109] Disruption did not wholly cease with the end of the civil war. The arrival, for example, of Francis Stewart, fifth Earl Bothwell in April 1589 with 600 horse and other troops must have had some impact on the town, even though his visit was only brief.[110]

Throughout the sixteenth century, the townspeople found themselves involved in the provision of labour and supplies further afield than Dalkeith. Oxen had to be supplied to pull the royal cannon in 1515.[111] Dalkeith men were instructed in April 1523 to be ready and correctly equipped to follow the signals of balls of fire, to defend their country against the English.[112] The people of Dalkeith were also to provide both corn for men and fodder for animals.[113] In 1549, men from Dalkeith, along with a workforce from other towns, were occupied in building a fort on Inchkeith Island, at a rate of two shillings a day for sixteen days.[114] In 1560, instructions were given that the inhabitants of Dalkeith, along with other towns, were to prepare 'bread, drink, flesh, fish and all other necessities' and transport them to the French army, based in Fife.[115] Five years later, a messenger to Dalkeith declared that all baxters, brewers, fleshers, cadgers and other food suppliers were to build up their stock and follow the army, to provision it.[116] A year later, it was horses that were requisitioned.[117] Troops at Stirling in 1584 needed food rations. Dalkeith, along with other Lothian and Fife towns, was instructed to supply 'baith hors meit and mannis meit'.[118]

Proximity to Edinburgh **figure 9** brought both advantage and disadvantage for Dalkeith. In 1585, Dalkeith's provost, bailies and council, along with those of other burghs, were invited to deliberate in Edinburgh and offer advice on the nature of

figure 9
Extract from J Blaeu's *Plan of Lothian and Linlitqvo*, mid seventeenth century

legislation to counteract outbreaks of the plague.[119] When plague hit Dalkeith, Edinburgh gave £20 to its relief, and three months later, when a new outbreak of infection struck, two Edinburgh representatives were delegated to visit the town and assess the problem.[120]

Edinburgh could, on occasion, be a somewhat overbearing neighbour. In 1604, for example, the inhabitants of Dalkeith, Musselburgh and other nearby towns complained bitterly that Edinburgh had imposed new levies on produce taken into or out of the capital: on every import of ale eight pence, of coal four pence, of food four pence, of fish or meat eight pence; and on every load taken out of Edinburgh four pence. This was a heavy burden on satellite towns that largely depended on the Edinburgh market for their well-being. The privy council appears to have considered this an undue burden; the impost was reduced to one penny per load.[121]

Equally, Edinburgh's need for supplies from the surrounding towns could also make the capital vulnerable. Bread was a basic necessity. Markets were held every Monday, Wednesday and Friday; and Dalkeith baxters were amongst those who benefited from this outlet. There arose a suspicion, however, that sub-standard bread was being imported from the neighbouring burghs, on the guarantee of a sale. On 14 April 1608, the bailies of Edinburgh were therefore authorised to test the quality of all bread brought to sale at their market.[122] The following year a step further was taken; the medieval practice of monitoring both quality and weight of bread was reinstated.[123]

The importance of communication with neighbouring burghs, and Edinburgh in particular, is highlighted by the concern for maintenance of roads and bridges. An act of parliament of 1594 specifically dealt with the issue of mending and maintaining the two bridges at Dalkeith, the north one over the North Esk (Lugton Bridge) and the south one over the South Esk (Cow Bridge), which were 'now almaist decayed'.[124] The current siting of the Lugton Bridge is a little up river from the original.[125] A number of towns and villages, including Dalkeith, petitioned the privy council in 1595, for example, for permission to raise a toll for the repair of the 'brig and calsay [cobbled street]' called the Lady Brigend, near Edinburgh.[126] This necessity for ready access was summed up in 1614, when a licence was given to the community and inhabitants of Dalkeith 'to uplift a tax for the repairing of bridges north and south of the town which [were] in danger of being carried away by the ice and snow from the heights, which will be of great inconvenience in respect of the great traffic over them to Edinburgh, and from the same to all parts of the realm lately called the Borders'. Carts were to pay two pence Scots and horses that were led, one penny. Interestingly, and unusually, this toll had to be paid not only on crossing the bridges, but also if traversing the rivers by the nearest fords to the bridges.[127]

It is possible, from the records, to begin to gain a picture of the townscape and life in the town for the ordinary burgess and indweller, whose existence was very different from that in the castle/palace. Dalkeith Palace and parks dominated the townscape. Nearby stood the earl's woods, which were enclosed by a wall in 1619.[128] Dalkeith town was essentially still one street, called the High Street, running from east to west, away from the castle.[129] A number of vennels or wynds ran from the High Street. A vennel or lane, called the South Vennel or sometimes the Common Vennel,[130] ran southwards from the High Street, much on the alignment of present-day South Street. The West Wynd also ran southwards from the High Street, a little further west than South Vennel.[131] From the north side of the High Street another vennel led to Lugton Bridge, the main crossing point of the River North Esk, en route to Edinburgh.[132]

There was by now a tolbooth in the town, and it is safe to assume that it stood near the market cross at the wide market place.[133] The tolbooth, along with the market cross, was the most important secular building in the town. It was here that market dues were collected, the town weights were kept, burgh council meetings were held and the gaol was housed. To the south of the High Street, also near the site of the cross, stood an old kiln,[134] which was demolished by 1608.[135] There was more than one school in the town by

figure 10
Nineteenth-century view of St Nicholas Church, with charity workhouse (now demolished)

1584, as, in this year, John Ker was gifted the altarage of St John the Baptist, for the support he had given 'the sculeis' over the previous seven years.[136] Moreover, Mr Andrew Alane was a schoolmaster in Dalkeith in 1582,[137] which also suggests more than one schoolmaster. It was decided in 1591, however, that for the duration of Mr George Hastie's time in Dalkeith there should be only one school and that the 'bairnes' should be encouraged to return to it; which implies that rivalry between schools and absenteeism had arisen.[138] A hospice, supported by the provost of St Nicholas Church, stood on the north side of the High Street **figure 10**.[139] The town also had more than one mill by 1540,[140] one of which was called the Pow Mill.[141] At least one of these mills was supplied by water controlled by the 'water yett' that stood on the Hauch of Dalkeith, by a little oak tree on the way to Braehead.[142] On 1 December 1583, it is recorded that the rentals of the corn mills of Dalkeith were £200, a not insignificant sum,[143] and by 1587, there were four grain and cloth mills in Dalkeith.[144]

Lining the street were the tenements and burgage plots of the burgesses. It is interesting that these plots were commonly called 'cottage lands',[145] 'cotlands',[146] 'cottage tenements',[147] 'husbandlands'[148] or 'husband tenements',[149] rather than tofts, rigs, or burgage plots, as is the norm in burghs of this period. This is probably a reflection of the predominantly agricultural nature of the town. Many of the townspeople leased acres of land, such as Thorniecruiks,[150] Corsfurlanddaillis,[151] Stanelawis,[152] Litstans-croft (thirteen acres),[153] Kingis-furde,[154] Ramsayis-croft,[155] the Steill (twenty-six acres),[156] Brewlandis[157] and Langside[158] in the vicinity of the town. The farmed land was laid out in rigs.[159] Aerial photography shows up broad rig in the grounds of Dalkeith estate, in the area now called Steel Park **figure 3**. This is, in all probability, the land called 'the Steill' in the sixteenth century, but the land may have been laid out in rigs in earlier centuries. Evidently a clearance was effected after the sixteenth century. Some of the corn sold at the weekly corn market, held on a Sunday until 1581, when it was transferred to a Tuesday, would have been grown by the burgesses on these acres of land.[160] By this time Dalkeith was, without doubt, functioning as a market centre for many rural settlements in the vicinity.

Other markets were clearly still being held on a Sunday, as in 1583 the Edinburgh magistrates enacted that none of their burgesses should attend any Sunday markets in neighbouring towns, including Dalkeith.[161] The markets were not only for the sale and purchase of victuals. The local craftsmen, such as the cutler, John Lytoun, an indweller in the town in 1576,[162] the wrights who were also employed on the crown's business,[163] the coopers[164] and the smiths[165] would also sell their products. The town also had the right to hold a fair, which would attract merchants from much further afield in Scotland, and from abroad. From 1581, its appointed date was 10 October.[166] Some of the townspeople probably also found employment as quarriers of coal on the Dalkeith estate,[167] as gardeners, as general odd job men,[168] and as washer women. A number of the residents must have worked as millers; and the town obviously had numerous baxters, brewers, fleshers and cadgers, necessary not only to supply the palace, but also the army (*see* p 23).

There is no evidence that the town was encircled with walls, although many medieval Scottish towns surrounded themselves with ditches and palisading. It is quite probable that this was the case also in Dalkeith, perhaps at the foot of the burgage plots. This would provide at least a psychological, if not a highly defensible physical barrier. Entrance to and exit from the town would have been either through small gates at the back of the burgage plots or through the main gates, or ports, of the town. The existence of a West Port in 1599, outside which building was under way, might, by its very name, imply that there was also an East Port.[169] It is known that there were gates of iron at Dalkeith by 1550, but whether these were the gates to the castle, which had at least fore and back gates,[170] or to the town is unclear.[171] If they were the town ports, precisely where they were sited at this time is unknown.

The fabric of the town must have suffered greatly from the frequent burnings and ravages (*see* p 23). St Nicholas Church was also to undergo change after the Reformation. The choir was sealed off and abandoned in 1590, as a 'monument of idolatry';[172]

although the collegiate church still technically had a provost in 1593.[173] The western part continued to function as the parish church **figure 10**. In 1591, it was in poor material state, although the congregation and minister declared themselves willing to repair it.[174] In 1594, a platform was built on the steeple;[175] its main purpose was to 'bear ane brassen piece';[176] whether this is a reference to a cannon or extra roofing is unclear. It is unlikely to have been a decorative addition, unless it is associated with the bells which are known to have been in use.[177] Major transformation work was undertaken in the interior, including the insertion of some lofts, or seats, for the incorporated crafts.[178]

The records also offer an insight into the need and method of social control in the town in the sixteenth century. Lesser offences would have been met with a fine and public humiliation in the stocks or jougs, as in other burghs. More serious offences were dealt with by incarceration in the burgh tolbooth, and more serious still by banishment or imprisonment in Edinburgh's tolbooth. It appears, however, that punishment was not always justified. Three men from Dalkeith, for example, successfully appealed against their imprisonment for no reason, in Dalkeith tolbooth, by the two bailies of the regality, Robert Porteous and James Douglas in 1591.[179] But, equally, some burgesses and indwellers themselves ignored the due course of justice. A Dalkeith couple had been instructed to remove themselves, their tenants, subtenants and cottars from a property, a manse and yard that formed part of the prebendary of Ingliston. This was ignored and they were put to the horn (outlawed). In spite of this, they 'proudly and contemptuously remained at the horn as yet unrelaxed dwelling in Dalkeith, and haunting kirks, markets and other places as if they were free subjects'. They were warded in Edinburgh tolbooth for their trouble.[180]

Witchcraft was a 'crime' on the increase. It had already been noted, in 1591, that one of those involved in the North Berwick witch trial came from Dalkeith.[181] In 1609 Janet Drysdale, for example, was accused of murder by witchcraft in the presbytery of Dalkeith.[182] The outcome is not known, but was unlikely to have been in her favour. Breach of the peace sometimes resulted in near murder. Janet Langton, while walking from Dalkeith to Newbattle in April 1610, was assaulted, she claimed, by George Steven of Dalkeith. He attacked her 'with a grite trie forkit with irne, broke two of her ribs and left her for dead'.[183] Dalkeith also witnessed attacks on greater personages than widows; an attempt was made to kill the minister of Dalkeith in the graveyard in 1615.[184] A royal messenger, while proclaiming letters at the market cross of Dalkeith in 1612, did not receive due courtesy. One Archibald Smebaird, a maltman in Dalkeith,

> *came behind his back and gave him sundry blows on the head ... took the said letters from him, rave the signet from them and threw them together like a glove and put them in his pocket, and then he gripped the said [messenger] by the middle, and with great force and violence through [sic] him from the highest step of the cross to the ground, so that, landing upon his head, he was very ill hurt, and so astonished with the fall, and hurt of his head, he was for a long time without breath or speach.*

The maltman was committed to Edinburgh tolbooth.[185] Even Robert Maxwell, first earl of Nithsdale and confidante of Charles I (1625–49), had his coach held up in Dalkeith, although this rabbling may have been stirred up by nobles whose vested interests in kirklands and teinds were under threat from the king's policies.[186]

the seventeenth century

After the Union of the Crowns, in 1603, and the departure of the Scottish monarchs to London, Dalkeith was to see royalty more rarely. James VI visited, however, on at least two occasions in 1617, on his return to Scotland. Preparations were being made for his arrival in Scotland in March, when Dalkeith was instructed to provide twenty fed horses for the use of the king's household. Other towns were likewise requisitioned: Musselburgh, for example, had to provide twelve horses, Stirling forty and Glasgow 300.[187] In May, Dalkeith had to supply six carts, each with four horses, to transport the king's train from Seton to Holyrood. Many more horses and carts were requisitioned from other towns.[188] On 11 June, the king, having left Edinburgh at 4 am, was at Dalkeith for 'his recreation and pleasure'. Eight pieces of Latin verse, called 'The Muses' Welcome',[189] were presented to him. He was back again in July, this time staying four days.[190] The townspeople would have been well used to the sight of nobility passing up their High Street to the palace gates. The English nobles who were entertained at Dalkeith in 1619 must have been considered of great importance. The Earl of Morton was permitted to borrow as much of the royal silver plate as he required for this visit.[191]

Charles I spent a night at the palace during his progress to Edinburgh in June 1633.[192] Preparations were made well in advance: Dalkeith, along with other burghs, had been asked in the previous December how many nolts (cows) they could supply for this visit.[193] It is not surprising that King Charles should stay overnight so near to Edinburgh, as William, eighth earl of Morton, was a great favourite, holding the offices and titles of Privy Purse, Captain of the Guard, Lord Treasurer of Scotland and Knight of the Noble Order of the Garter.[194] Indeed, Charles I found Dalkeith Palace and estate sufficiently attractive that, in 1637, he wished to purchase it, in order to turn the 8,000 acres into a deer park. The transaction, however, was never concluded.[195] A year later, in the wake of unrest over liturgy, the privy council moved from Linlithgow, having virtually abandoned the capital the previous year, to Dalkeith; and even the 'Honours of Scotland' were housed at Dalkeith for a while, before their return to Edinburgh.[196]

Scotland was about to enter into, in effect, a nationalist revolt which had, along with a religious purpose, a political agenda. Dalkeith would often be near the centre of the storm over the following two decades. The parish church, for example, fared badly, as did many others, being used by the leader of the Independents, Oliver Cromwell, as a military barracks and stable for his horses, after the defeat of the Scots at Dunbar on 3 September 1650. The Dalkeith area was suspected of harbouring royalists. Oliver Cromwell, writing to the governor of Borthwick Castle in 1650, commented that 'one nest of mosstroopers, not far off in the Dalkeith region, ought specially to be abated'.[197] There is evidence of some plundering of Dalkeith Palace by the English, but sufficient remained of the silver and plenishings for an inventory to be made in 1650.[198]

Another change in the old order was the passing of the ownership of Dalkeith to the Buccleuch family in 1642, when Francis, second earl of Buccleuch, purchased the palace and estate from the eighth earl of Morton, for 'a very high price'.[199] Morton was forced to sell Dalkeith, along with other estates, in order to settle huge debts. A zealous royalist, Buccleuch was fined £200,000 for his allegiance when the Commonwealth was established. His death, in 1651, left two daughters as heiresses. The older daughter, Mary, succeeded to the estate as Countess of Buccleuch in her own right. Being only a child, there was much intriguing and early marriage plans, and the advice of Cromwell himself was sought. As a result, the Cromwellian officer who was later to become the Commander-in-Chief in Scotland, Lieutenant General Monck, was appointed as her guardian. It was to Dalkeith that all the Scottish and English commissioners of shires were called in 1651 to assent to the Cromwellian Union. Scottish commissioners arrived in the town from the February of 1652, the English having arrived the previous month.[200] Not all those who arrived, however, supported the cause. Lauchlan Mackintosh, brother to the laird of Mackintosh, representing Inverness-shire, for example, refused to denounce the king in exchange for the offices of sheriff and commissary of Inverness-shire.[201] Colonel Robert Lilburne, the Commander-in-Chief of the forces in Scotland, was based in Dalkeith in 1653.[202]

The links of Monck with Dalkeith were to be close, as he leased the palace for five years from 1654,[203] paying as rental £110 for the park and a mere three pence annually for the palace. The commissioners, on the other hand, had paid no rental during their stay earlier in the decade,[204] but goods left by them in Dalkeith Palace were put up for sale in 1653.[205] It was to be at Dalkeith that Monck would bury one of his children in

February 1657. The hierarchy of the town would doubtless have been involved, paying their respects, since it is known that the bailies and part of the council of Edinburgh also attended the funeral at Dalkeith.[206] The death of Mary, countess of Buccleuch was to follow four years later. Once again, the office bearers and many of the council of Edinburgh attended the funeral, and presumably so did the Dalkeith officials.[207] Countess Mary was to be succeeded by her sister, Anne.

Occupation by officials of the Protectorate may have been one factor in the adequate upkeep of the furbishings of Dalkeith Palace during these disturbed times. It was considered to be of sufficient luxury that it was emptied to furnish Holyroodhouse for Charles II (1660–85) in 1663.[208] There were to be close links between royalty and the Buccleuch family. The Duchess Anne married the son of Charles II, James, duke of Monmouth. A room in Dalkeith Palace was lavishly furnished for this occasion, entirely at the expense of Charles II.[209] On 20 April 1663, the young couple were created Duke and Duchess of Buccleuch and Earl and Countess of Dalkeith.[210]

Dalkeith and the Buccleuch family, however, were not to be immune from national events thereafter. Troops were frequently quartered in the town in the years between 1665 and 1669;[211] and remained there on an intermittent basis throughout the next decade.[212] Three companies of soldiers were quartered in the town in 1678.[213] The following year it was noted in the records of the privy council that the Duke of Buccleuch's tenants had been 'very great sufferers by quarterings upon them ... for eighteen years last past'. It was maintained that troops had been 'unequally quartered upon them, any part of the country besides'.[214] While there appears from the records to have been a brief respite for Dalkeith, by 1684 the town was again forced to be host to troops, and yet again in 1685.[215] In 1688 the town was once more housing the militia.[216] The Duke of Monmouth and Buccleuch was beheaded for treachery in 1685, on the instruction of James VII & II (1685–89).

A change of monarch, in the persons of William of Orange (1689–1702) and his wife, Mary II (1689–94), did not bring stability to Scotland. Yet again, Dalkeith would see itself pulled into national events and in 1690, for example, troops were quartered at Dalkeith, just as they were at Musselburgh and Leith.[217] The cumulative effect on the lives of the Dalkeith townspeople of the draining of material and emotional resources by the billeting of troops throughout this century is not documented, but may readily be guessed at.

Religious events, as well as political ones, disrupted the lives of the Dalkeith people. The congregation of St Nicholas Church, like those of Tranent and Duddingston, was swelled in 1622 by Edinburgh parishioners who objected to kneeling at communion.[218] One crime the presbytery was determined to eradicate was witchcraft. There were numerous cases of trial of witches held in Dalkeith, either before the bailie of Dalkeith regality court,[219] or before one or all of the town's four bailies.[220] By 1628, trials had been so frequent that the presbytery appealed to the privy council that the expense was such that they had been forced to take money 'out of the box of the poor'. This would be extremely hurtful to the poor 'who [were] more in number than all the contributors of their box can sustain'.[221] Various crimes were laid at the doors of witches. In 1628, for example, two women witches were accused of causing the death of Robert, second earl of Lothian.[222] Prior to trial and execution witches were kept in the tolbooth of Dalkeith, but from 1629, when William, the sixth earl of Morton, needed all the space in the tolbooth for 'the delinquents in his own regality',[223] other places of incarceration were found; one such was 'a little house abone the end of Newbattle kirk', but this proved insecure and leave was asked to remove the witch (Michael Erskine) to Edinburgh.[224] There was little relaxation of witch hunting; one of the most diligent in pursuit was the parish minister from 1659 to 1680, Rev William Calderwood,[225] who is commemorated in a plaque in St Nicholas Church (*see* pp 51–2 *&* 81). His zeal brought a number of witches to trial in Dalkeith.[226]

Although the records give few other insights into the townscape and the life of the ordinary people of Dalkeith in the seventeenth century, it is patently clear that both could not but be affected by national events, sitting as Dalkeith was, almost centre stage in the political arena. The impression is of an urban setting changing little in the seventeenth century from the previous one. The street pattern remained, it seems, the same; and cotlands[227] and husbandlands each side of the High Street continued to be let out, as well as larger stretches of land further afield, such as the Cross Acre and the East Acre, which lay to the east of the Cow Bridge,[228] the Thorniecruiks,[229] and Ramsayis Croft, which lay near the West Port of Dalkeith.[230]

The two bridges needed regular maintenance. There were ongoing repairs in the earlier half of the century,[231] and measures such as taking tolls from those using either the bridge or ford (unspecified) were, again, instituted in 1631.[232] Two years later, the shire commissioners were requested to ride the road from Dalkeith to Edinburgh to consider where they felt it should be enlarged or repaired, such was the importance of the thoroughfare.[233] In 1663, parliament recognised the strategic importance of these two crossings over the Esk, both for locals and strangers, as this was the main route from the south of the kingdom to Edinburgh. Permission was given for tolls to be raised for fifteen years to facilitate repair, since the bridges had been almost undermined by 'great inundations of water' in 1659 and since that time they were 'daylie decaying and [would] shortly fall to the ground'. It is clear that the commodities whose weight caused most damage were to be targeted: millstones, cart loads, horse loads of coal, lime, victual and ale, and sheep, cattle and horses en route to market.[234] By 1680, it is recorded that the Dalkeith–Edinburgh route was once again in poor condition.[235]

The palace (castle) and park of Dalkeith would have continued to dominate the landscape. It is unclear when a large stone boundary wall between town and castle was erected. In 1619 a contract was made for a wall to be built round the wood of Dalkeith; but there is no mention of the park surrounding the castle in this document.[236] When the lordship, barony and regality of Dalkeith was transferred to Francis, earl of Buccleuch, in 1642, it was described as 'extensive lands, lordship, regality, town and burgh of barony and regality of Dalkeith with its liberties, with the castle, gardens, orchards, forests and parks, grain and cloth mills, fisheries, rabbit warrens, tenants, coal mines, prebendary and patronage of the collegiate church'.[237] Twenty-two years later, when the same was granted to James, duke of Monmouth and Buccleuch, the lordship was similarly described, but the policies around the castle were specified as 'all the lands included within the stone dyke of the ... park'.[238] Clearly the castle was enclosed with a stone wall by 1664, but whether it had been so for decades or even centuries before is uncertain.

Equally unclear is whether the original route to the Cow Bridge was more direct than that seen on eighteenth-century maps, the latter following very much the present Musselburgh Road. If one may rely on Blaeu's seventeenth-century plan showing Dalkeith **figure 9**, based much on the work of Timothy Pont who was recording in the late sixteenth century, the route from the town to the South Esk was apparently more direct. The artificial bend of Musselburgh Road on eighteenth-century maps **figure 11**, respecting the wall of the Dalkeith Parks and forcing a circuitous route to the bridge, might suggest that the wall was a later feature and that there was originally a more direct route—this latter denied by its incorporation into the Dalkeith Parks and the building of a wall. A stray reference to the resignation of a tenement on the south side of the High Street, in 1556, throws an interesting light on this question. The resignation was effected at the green of Dalkeith. According to the evidence of this charter, the green was 'near the castle'.[239] But the topography of the town was such that there was no space for open public ground at the castle end of the High Street. The only available open ground was between where the Duke's Gates now stand and the castle itself. It is possible that here there is evidence of a town green, used by the public, as was the custom in other towns; but which was lost to the ducal policies, perhaps at the time of the extension of the castle in the time of Morton (*see* p 22 or sometime in the seventeenth century. The timing may also coincide with the enclosure of the Steill lands, once cultivated by the burgesses (*see* p 26).

It is known, however, that town and palace retained relatively close contact. The remnants of seventeenth-century housing may still be seen in the form of blocked

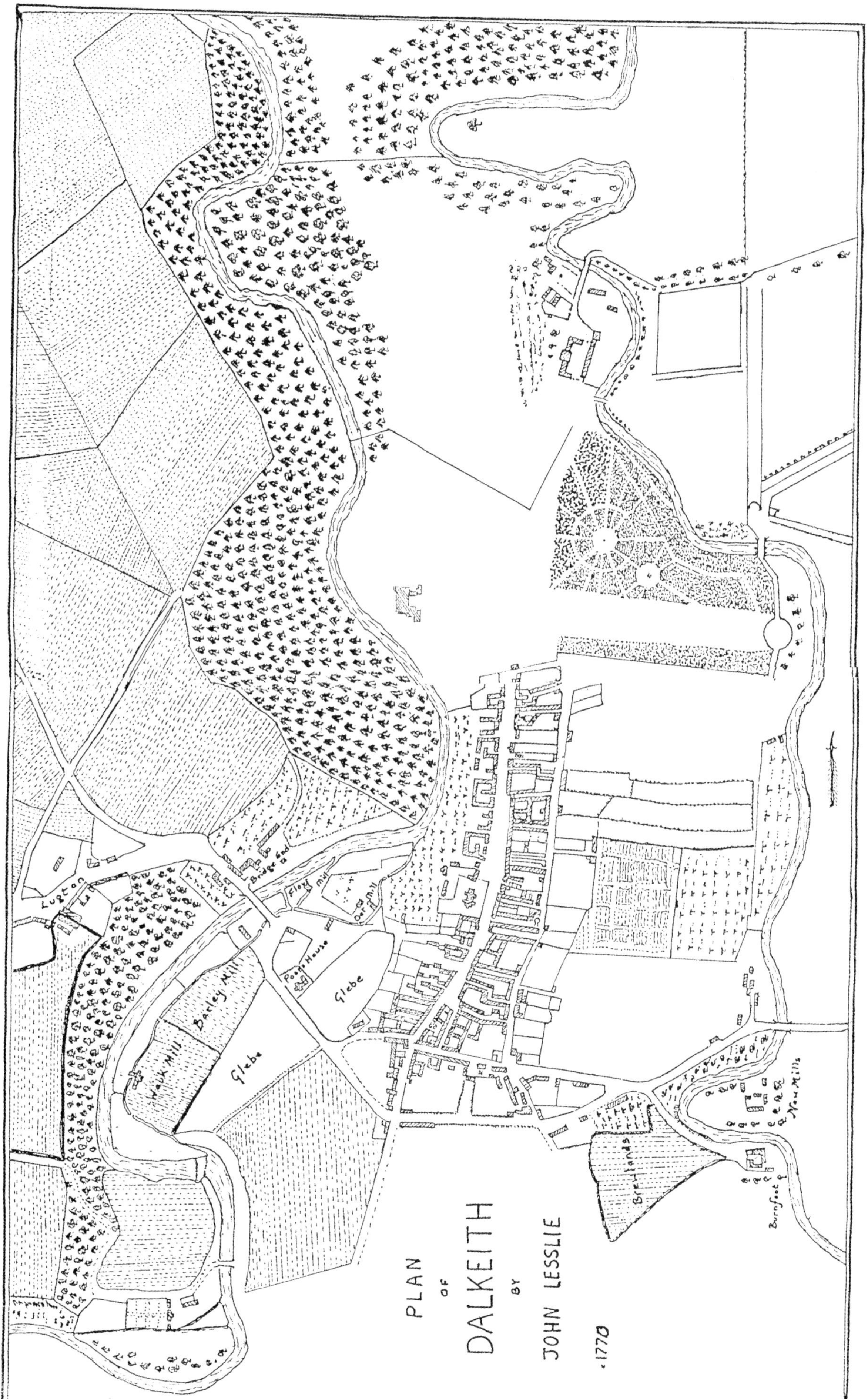

figure 11
Redrawing of a *Plan of Dalkeith* by John Lesslie, *c* 1770

figure 12
The tolbooth *left*, photographed in 1966

windows and doors in the south wall close by the present Duke's Gates at the head of the High Street (*see* p 82). Another seventeenth-century standing building is the tolbooth **figure 12**. Facing the wide market place, it was built in the later part of the century. The use of the sacristy of St Nicholas Church as a prison in 1675 might be indication of ongoing building works at the tolbooth, the traditional prison, at this time.[240] The date panel, 1648, above the tolbooth entrance is misleading, as this stonework was found on the Dalkeith estate in the eighteenth century and placed on the tolbooth only then. Dalkeith had had a tolbooth from at least the sixteenth century (*see* p 25), which was still functioning in 1647.[241] Whether it fell into disrepair and was partially or wholly replaced is unclear. Fairs and weekly markets seem to have continued throughout the century, in spite of the upheaval of billeted troops and the like. Occasional crises, such as plague in Preston and Prestonpans, meant that the markets and fairs of Dalkeith, along with those of Haddington, Preston and Tranent, were banned for some six weeks in 1636.[242]

Dalkeith had also had a school from at least the previous century. From 1622 to 1647, however, it was claimed that there was none functioning in the town, due to lack of funds. Following the 1646 Founding of Schools Act, Francis, the second earl of Buccleuch, opened a new school.[243] It was probably this same one that was noted in the privy council records in 1680 as taking in boarders.[244]

In 1660, after the misuse of the Cromwellian period and natural deterioration, the parish church was made wind- and water-tight.[245] Since the turn of the century the interior had housed some lofts of the local craftsmen (*see* p 27). A loft for the Earl of Buccleuch had been erected in 1645; and from 1660 there was a rapid escalation in the construction of lofts. In the west of the church were the lofts of the baxters, fleshers, dyers, weavers and the common lofts; to the north the tailors' loft; to the north-west, the merchants and skinners; and to the south the hammermen. The shoemakers had their loft below that of the merchants and the scholars beneath the tailors. These were under construction until 1838 when the colliers' loft was erected in the chancel. All would be demolished in the huge renovations that were undertaken in 1851,[246] but their previous existence remains an interesting comment on the range of crafts in seventeenth- and eighteenth-century Dalkeith.

In 1619, the tradesmen of Dalkeith were assessed somewhat dismissively as 'consisting of maltmen and labourers of the ground, who have no other trade, calling, handling or industry'. This harsh comment was made, however, during a dispute between Lanark and Dalkeith, when Dalkeith was refusing to buy new weights for its market from Lanark. It is noteworthy that Dalkeith's defence for this non-purchase was that it, like Tranent, was supplied by Edinburgh with all goods that were sold by weight and, therefore, had no need of new weights.[247] This was probably an exaggeration, but Dalkeith's dependency on Edinburgh is indisputable.

Closeness to the capital with its prominence of professions and specialist crafts probably meant there was little need for practitioners of law, printers or wig makers in Dalkeith. This is confirmed by the Poll Tax Returns of the 1690s.[248] Of a pollable male population of 1,180, only 2.5 per cent were involved in the professional services. Allied with a mere 1.8 per cent of landowners and gentlemen, it is immediately apparent that the vast majority of Dalkeith males were involved in humbler occupations. The town did have a number of merchants,[249] 5.8 per cent being so employed. In a sample thirty-seven towns, nineteen had a higher ratio of merchants and seventeen fewer, which suggests that Dalkeith was not unusual. It is significant that in 1693, when the royal burghs offered to share foreign trading rights with burghs of barony, market towns and other 'unfree places', in exchange for relief of 10 per cent of their land tax, Dalkeith took up the option.[250] While the project was marred by haggling over the price of admission and was never a great success, it is evidence, at least, of intent on the part of Dalkeith (*see also* pp 35–6).

It is not surprising to find that 12.8 per cent of Dalkeith men were employed in agriculture, although there may be an element of rural population included in the Dalkeith returns which would exaggerate the agricultural figures. The glimpses of the townscape that come through the records are strong indication that Dalkeith was still essentially rural, with much of the burgh lands set out for cultivation or pasture. By far the greatest proportion of workers, 59.2 per cent, however, were involved in manufacture. When the manufactures are broken down, a telling overview of the town's occupational structure is gained: 24.9 per cent were involved in textiles, 14.5 per cent in clothing, 11.8 per cent in leather, 5.4 per cent in metal, 12.6 per cent in wood and construction, and 30.7 per cent in food and drink. The high proportion of textile workers is probably indicative of the demand for cloth from the capital, weaving taking place in the town, as it did in Musselburgh, before transportation to Edinburgh for dyeing and tailoring.

Employment in the food and drink sector, likewise, was probably weighted by the Edinburgh market. Millers and bakers[251] would supply home demand, but there was also a substantial market to be found in the capital. A new bakehouse and granary was built to the north of the High Street, a little before 1673.[252] The number of fleshers in Dalkeith was unusually high. This was probably a reflection of the Edinburgh ruling that no slaughtering was allowed in the city. Animals were fattened near Dalkeith, sometimes having been reared in the Borders, by landowners such as the Buccleuchs; then brought into Dalkeith for slaughtering; and afterwards transported to Edinburgh as meat. It may be significant that little use was made of one by-product, the hides. There were relatively few leather workers in Dalkeith. It is quite possible that there is, here, evidence of judicious networking between Edinburgh's satellite towns—Musselburgh had a high proportion of leather workers. Another by-product was tallow. The Dalkeith candle-makers were sufficiently productive to be able to compete with the Edinburgh candlemakers in their own city.[253] The 5.4 per cent metal workers would have included a number of iron workers, iron working having been established in Dalkeith since at least 1648 (*see also* p 34). That the trades of Dalkeith were proactive is suggested by the fact that they were electing deacons of their individual crafts. They fell foul of central government in 1683, however, by failing to test the skills of their prospective apprentices.[254]

the eighteenth century

The century was to open with extensive building works at Dalkeith. On her return from England, Anne, duchess of Buccleuch, set about upgrading the family home; Morton's castle/palace was rebuilt almost in its entirety between 1702 and 1711, although some sixteenth-century features were retained. James Smith was commissioned to design and effect these alterations. The south-eastern courtyard wall was demolished, and parts of the earlier building were absorbed, particularly in the south-western corner and probably also in the north and west wings. This new U-plan mansion had one of the earliest classical façades in Scotland, with an entrance with giant Corinthian pilasters over which is an enormously deep, bracketed pediment. All the roofs are bellcast in shape. Dalkeith Palace was transformed into one of the grandest of the early classical houses in Scotland.

Further modifications were made in 1762–3, when repair and refacing were undertaken by John Adam; it is possible that some of the detailed richness comes from this time. Later in the century, in the 1780s, a few alterations were effected, including the addition of a bow-windowed library in the east range, by William Playfair.

The lavishness of the interior and the trappings that accompanied this transformation were of equal grandeur. The formal entrance and public apartments, with their marble doorcases and carved cornices, are among the grandest examples in Scotland. Duchess Anne's own apartments in the north-east corner of the palace were the most richly decorated. A suite of three rooms—the anteroom, the boudoir and Duchess Anne's room—contains features such as a marble panel by Grinling Gibbons and two painted mirrors of the highest quality, probably brought from the duchess's seat in England, Moor Park.

The grounds surrounding the palace were likewise transformed, with avenues and vistas. Daniel Defoe, visiting some time before 1724, commented that in the park there were 'fine avenues, some already made and planted, others designed, but not yet finished; also there [were] to be waterworks, *jette d'eaus*, and a canal, but these [were] not yet laid out'.[255] The stables and coach-house were erected in 1740, to a design of William Adam. The complex was capable of accommodating about sixty horses, carriages and all the staff necessary to work them. Later in the century, the park would be softened by the informal plantings of Henry, third duke of Buccleuch and fifth duke of Queensberry. It was on his instruction that the Montagu Bridge, to the north-east end of the park, was erected in 1792. Designed by Robert Adam and constructed by his brother James, it originally had three life-sized stags on the parapet, but these were removed as they frightened the horses. The erection in 1784, by James Playfair, of the Duke's Gates would have made a strong visual impact on the populace, standing as they do at the head of the High Street, imposing definition on the separateness of estate and town.

These grand schemes must have affected the townspeople, although how much is unclear. Such extensive renovations would probably have depended on the skills of local craftsmen, masons, carpenters, slaters and the like; and on a workforce for casual labour, such as gardening or assistance in the classical laundry set up in the palace grounds. David Turner, resident in Dalkeith, for example, was working on the new park wall in 1726; and James Gray, who was repairing the old park wall in the same year, was probably also a local man.[256] It is known that the local iron mills were supplying the estate with iron gates, railings and tools in the mid eighteenth century. Another important product of the iron mills was iron clogs for the colliers who worked the nearby mines at Cowden, Smeaton and Sheriffhall;[257] and iron work was necessary in the town, for example for the Cow Bridge in 1727.[258] Two local men, Thomas Chaddock and Thomas Thomson, served as waggoners to Anne, duchess of Buccleuch; and George Cranstoun, the town carrier, and James Cleghorn, who had two carts with wheels and two without, two old horses and two old mares, were probably all called into service on occasion.[259]

Dalkeith was also gaining a reputation for its woollen manufacture. On 27 August 1743, a manufacturing house was set up in Kilmarnock.[260] It is interesting that this production of coarse fabrics, carpets, duffles, blankets and plaids was introduced by a Mary Gardiner, who brought spinners and weavers of carpets from Dalkeith, which was by then renowned for its woollen products.[261] Richard Pococke, while on one of his tours of Scotland in 1760, noted that Dalkeith had a linen manufactory.[262] Although the *Old Statistical Account* commented that there was only a little manufacturing in the town, a tannery and soap works were noted. The town's candlemaking was considered of high quality and in 1790 a tambour, or drum, factory was established.[263] Clearly, Dalkeith was now taking some advantage of the by-products of the cattle that were still regularly driven to its markets (*see* p 33). The remains of the eighteenth-century skinnery can still be seen in the industrial estate at Grannies Park.

The baxters continued to form an important part of the local economy; and in 1749 their incorporation petitioned Francis, second duke of Buccleuch, for replacement of the common stones for grinding with marble ones, so that they could better meet the competition of neighbouring mills, who were getting better results with marble stones.[264] The plan of Dalkeith, drawn by John Lesslie *c* 1770 **figure 11**, indicates the importance of the mills in the town. Both the North and South Esk rivers provided water power. A barley mill, flour mill and oat mill are depicted drawing water from the North Esk, as well as a waulk mill. The flour mill can still be seen in Grannies Park. An L-shaped building of three storeys and a loft, the attached cartshed is a little later in date; but the arched mill race depicted on the map is still visible. On the South Esk, there was a complex of buildings, called the Newmills. A remnant of these is still standing (*see* p 69). These, too, were built in the eighteenth century, but replaced earlier mills which may have been in existence from the twelfth or thirteenth centuries, called the Old Mills.

It is not surprising that there should have been so many grain mills and ancillary buildings in the town. Apart from the obvious natural geographical advantage of a superb water supply, it was said of Dalkeith, in 1724, that it was a 'pretty large market-town, and the better market for being so near to Edinburgh; for there comes great quantities of provisions here from the southern countries, which are brought up here to be carried to Edinburgh market again, and sold there'.[265] One of the most important commodities brought to Dalkeith was grain. Indeed, it was said that Dalkeith was 'perhaps the greatest grain market in Scotland', and that this grain, once sold, brought 'ready' money, which the farmers then spent in the town. Some of the grain was transported to the west, to supply such towns as Carron, Glasgow and Paisley. Clearly this weekly market, held on a Thursday, functioned as an important distribution point not only for the capital. As well as this Thursday market, there was also a meal market, held every Monday from Martinmas to Whitsun.[266]

Dalkeith's role as a market was reinforced by its weekly cattle market, held every Tuesday. This brought not merely stock farmers to the town with money to spend, but also provided the town's butchers with the necessary animals to supply the Edinburgh market. On some occasions, it was said, the consumers in the capital took all the meat the Dalkeith butchers could kill.[267] The local craftsmen also took some advantage of the by-products of the butchers' activities (*see* p 34). As well as this weekly market, the town also held an annual fair on the third Tuesday of October. This catered largely for the trade in horses and black cattle.[268]

The records suggest that co-operation between neighbouring burghs was acceptable, even to the point of opposition to Edinburgh's centralising policy. In 1715, for example, when Musselburgh decided to change the date of its St Loretto fair, it had this fact announced in both Dalkeith and Haddington,[269] as appears to have been the case in the previous century.[270] Thirteen years later, as the Dalkeith market was held on a Thursday and many Musselburgh residents attended, the Musselburgh council changed its court day from Thursday to Tuesday.[271] In 1729, Edinburgh decided to hold a new weekly corn market. The surrounding burghs clearly felt that their livelihood was threatened, and that the corn market of Dalkeith would be undermined. This, in turn, would be disastrous for Musselburgh and its grain mills, which were partially fed by Dalkeith, and also for local heritors with mills on the Water of Esk. They therefore gave 'support to Dalkeith and the Duchess [of Buccleuch] and to other neighbours for preserving and maintaining [their] own rights and priviledges in support of a weekly market at Dalkeith'.[272]

Dalkeith's attempts to break into overseas trade do not appear to have met with much success. In 1705, the meeting of the committee of the Convention of Royal Burghs to deal with unfree trade and relieve the royal burghs of the weight of the tax roll, voted that Dalkeith should pay 2s yearly from 1697 to 1706.[273] This was a minuscule amount out of a notional £100; and is a measure of how little foreign trade Dalkeith was pursuing. In spite of the slightness of its contribution, Dalkeith, along with other towns, was to be prosecuted for deficiencies in payment in 1716.[274] Its quota, however, was raised from 2s to 3s in 1719 and to 4s in 1723, which might suggest some minor improvement.[275] Seven years later, an agent was appointed by the Convention of Royal Burghs to assist 'several traders' in Dalkeith in their lawsuit against the inhabitants of the town. An attempt was being made to force all to contribute to the payment of cess.[276] Whether their action was successful is unclear. Equally uncertain is the identity of these 'several traders'; while they may have been Dalkeith merchants, it is equally possible that amongst their numbers were some Edinburgh merchants.

The slight increase in representation of the professions in Dalkeith may also be accounted for by closeness to Edinburgh. In the first decade of the eighteenth century, for example, Sir William Calderwood, advocate, who was infeft of lands in Dalkeith, was without doubt practising in the capital. At the same time, Alexander Mein, surgeon, had a house and a half cot tenement near to the cross. He may have been using his skills in the town; indeed, since he, together with Benjamin Robinson, secretary to the duchess, witnessed a charter from Duchess Anne to Sir William Calderwood, in all probability he was surgeon to the duchess.[277] Not all who were infeft in land in Dalkeith should be assumed, however, to have made their living in the town. Dalkeith was quite close enough to the capital to be used as a dormitory base for professional groups, or merely as a means of extending land-holding. In 1771, for example, the Right Honourable Sir William Calderwood of Polton, senator to the College of Justice, had confirmed sasine of lands in Dalkeith that he had previously held.[278]

When an analysis was made in the 1790s of the occupational structure of the town, there was no mention of lawyers or advocates. The town did, however, reputedly have six physicians; they and five hairdressers and two watchmakers would suggest a certain level of sophistication in the burgh. There were also five clergymen and three university students. The remaining occupations, however, reflect the lifestyles of the vast majority of the people: weavers, fifty-six; weavers, not incorporated, twenty-one; shoemakers, sixty-two; tailors, forty-four; dyers, twelve; gardeners, fifty-three; butchers, thirty; candlemakers, three; hammermen, masons and wrights, seventy-seven; carters, sixty or seventy; farmers, eleven; bakers, thirty-six; and brewers, four.[279]

It has been estimated that there were 4,366 people in the parish by the 1790s. This was made up of 1,095 families, fifty of which were in the rural area; the rest were in Dalkeith, Lugton and Bridgend.[280] Given that there were still over 4,000 in Dalkeith, Lugton and Bridgend, the removal of the Lugton inhabitants would probably leave Dalkeith and Bridgend with a population somewhere between 3,500 and 4,000. Compared with Webster's 1755 figure, of 3,110 in the parish, there had been a significant increase in the population.[281]

Eighteenth-century maps suggest that this increase in population had little effect on the street pattern. In any town, the street lay-out is usually its most enduring topographical feature. The main street was by now fully built up, and there is cartographic evidence of repletion, or building in the backlands. This was more marked on the south side of the street than on the north, partly due to the fact that the land behind the street frontage on the north fell steeply down to the Esk. The back lane to the properties on the south side of the street was probably by now formalised into a more important thoroughfare, leading as it did straight into the Musselburgh Road; and there may have been some development on this new street, although it was not extensive. The Old Meal Market Inn on the south-west corner of the street is one such remnant **figure 13**. Closes running back from the High Street, on both sides, were now developed with dwellings and workshops. Brunton's Close by 115/117 High Street still retains many of its original characteristics and gives an insight into eighteenth-century Dalkeith. Visitors to Dalkeith commented favourably on the townscape. Daniel Defoe wrote in 1724 that the 'town [was] spacious, and well built, and [was] the better, no doubt, for the neighbourhood of so many noblemen's and gentlemen's houses of such eminence in the neighbourhood'.[282] By the end of the century, it was said of the town that it was 'though not a royal borough ... a considerable place ... it contain[ed] one very handsome street, beside lanes'.[283]

St Nicholas Church remained still the dominant visual impact. Contemporary records indicate that it was often under repair. The clock in the steeple, for example, was cleaned in 1724, and the main spring needed repair work four years later.[284] By 1752, however, the steeple was in a ruinous state and so dangerous that it had to be taken down. For its own

figure 13 The seventeenth-century Old Meal Market Inn

safety the congregation was obliged to worship in a field. Ten years later, a new steeple was erected and the old bells were replaced, all at a cost of £540 19s 8¾d.[285] Due to neglect, the roof of the old church, blocked off from the body of the church since the sixteenth century (*see* pp 26–7), fell in.[286]

By the end of the century there were various religious persuasions in Dalkeith, all with set places of worship, although these might often be private houses. They included Burghers, Antiburghers, Methodists and a Relief Church. There was also one family of Cameronians and another who were reputed to be Anabaptists.[287] It is known, also, that there was an Episcopalian minister in Dalkeith in 1714; and that he had a congregation, which Duchess Anne 'encouraged' and 'upheld'.[288] Whether they had a formal 'meeting house' or Episcopalian chapel, as was the case in Musselburgh by 1704, is unclear.[289]

The duchess also supported the poor of the parish. In her will of 1722 she left £100 sterling to be distributed amongst the poor by the bailie and minister.[290] This would, without doubt, have seemed a windfall to the poor, although in relation to other bequests, it was a fairly paltry sum. By the end of the century, between sixteen and eighteen poor were receiving kirk funds in the summer months, but this total rose in the winter months when there was no work to be had in the fields. A charity workhouse had also been set up by then, which could house up to forty inmates **figure 10**.[291] John Wood's plan of 1822 **figure 14** sites this immediately to the west of St Nicholas Church. According to Lesslie's plan of *c* 1770 **figure 11**, a poor house stood on the east side of the Old Edinburgh Road, north of the glebe, near to the Lugton Bridge. This was erected in 1747 by the Kirk Session.[292]

The glebe stretched on both sides of the Old Edinburgh Road and covered approximately six acres.[293] The manse was in need of repair in 1752, although the nature of the fault is not recorded. Built in 1681, it was not considered satisfactory by the end of the eighteenth century because of its situation: surrounded by buildings on three sides, it was effectively deprived of sunshine for half of the year.[294]

The grammar school, as well as the master's house, was sited behind the parish church. For much of the century it was considered to be one of the most celebrated in the country. It was attended by all classes of society, including children of aristocrats and local gentry. They included John Adam, the son of architect William Adam; Robert Smith from Lugton, who was to become a famous architect in Philadelphia; probably John Kay, the engraver; and many others. In 1729, repair work was being undertaken on the building at the expense of the Buccleuchs.[295] Mr Dykes, the headmaster, in 1710 owed money to the doctor for sundry medicines he had purchased for the scholars who boarded in his house. The debt was more often to the schoolmaster. In 1739, the rector, John Leslie, was awaiting payment of board, lodgings and washing provided for one Richard Lawson. The rector's successor, a Mr John Love, died in 1750, before receiving his dues from John Inglis

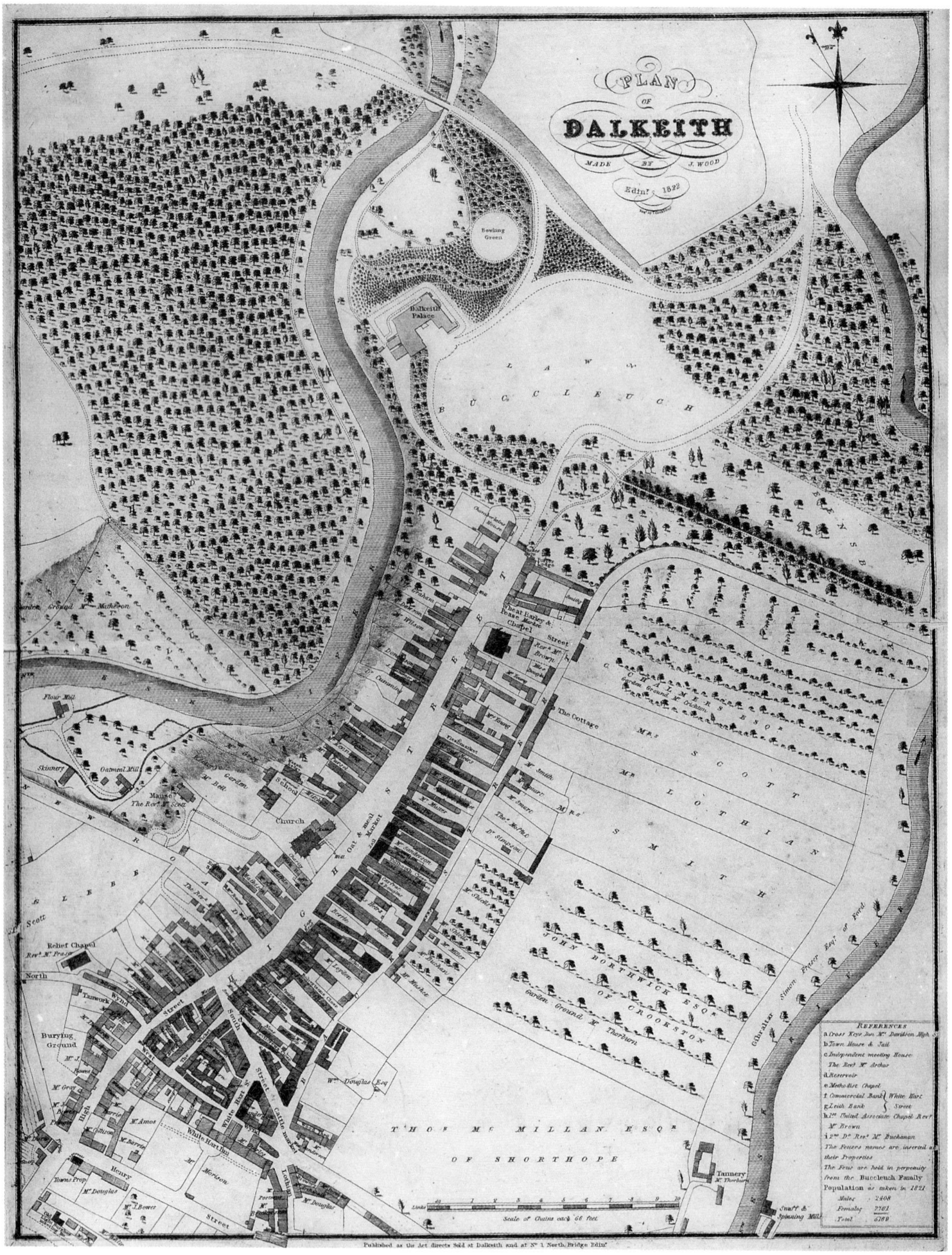

figure 14
John Wood's
Plan of Dalkeith
1822

of Auchendinny.[296] John Love had recommended, in 1741, that the school roof should be re-thatched or slated,[297] thus indicating that the school was thatched, as, indeed, many of the houses would have been at this time. The school was in need of tables and forms as well as windows in 1752;[298] but in 1774, it was reported by Lord President Forbes to his sister that the school was 'in very good order and the boys well taken care of. The whole expense for a year, including the masters fees and cloaths, [did] not exceed £25'.[299] For a while its reputation declined, but due to the diligence of rectors in the last decades of the century, its fame was somewhat restored. About twenty of the scholars boarded with the rector in the 1790s. By this time, there were also four English schools in the town, all of which were apparently well attended, one attracting as many as eighty to a hundred pupils.[300]

Public buildings, bridges and roadways were a constant drain on town finances, even though much was financed by the dukes of Buccleuch. In September 1725, for example, part of the highway near Bridgend was under repair;[301] a month later a hole in Lugton Bridge had to be patched;[302] four years later, work was being effected on the tolbooth;[303] the cemetery had to be maintained;[304] the weighhouse required maintenance in 1768;[305] and in the same year an ice house and slaughter house were built. The former would have been for Dalkeith House, perhaps the same as may still be seen in the grounds; but it is safe to assume that the slaughter house was for the benefit of the town, although its site is not known.[306]

A common sight in the town, as in the previous century, was the militia. The available evidence suggests that they were often involved in disturbances with local people. The butchers, for example, banded together against the troops billeted in their town; but the fracas resulted in the butchers' leader being clubbed to death with a musket. The verdict against the soldier who had been responsible was, however, 'not-proven'. It was also reported that soldiers broke into the yard of the minister, David Plenderleith, and struck his wife. The offenders were court martialled and sentenced to a whipping. The Kirk Session was at pains to prevent misdemeanours between local girls and soldiers. Christine Thomson, for example, was seen at Ironmill bank on a Saturday night before the Sunday sacrament in 1729. While she admitted she had been out for a 'drink', she denied going with the soldiers to the Ironmills, but in future she would 'walk more regularly to come home'.[307] Prince Charles Edward Stewart's troops 'concentrated at Dalkeith' on 31 October 1745, while the prince stayed at Pinkie House, Musselburgh. They were joined by him the next day and the prince lodged at Dalkeith House, the family being absent, before marching south to Lauder on 3 November.[308]

All was not hardship. There was often cause for happier times. In 1728, for example, the townspeople were provided with free ale to celebrate the king's birthday.[309] The town also had a piper and a drummer who led festivities.[310] Some of the standing buildings in Dalkeith are reminders of the fact that for some sections of Dalkeith society, life was increasingly genteel. *Nos* 1–5 and 6 London Road are fine examples of quality building, *nos* 1–3 being built for Dalkeith merchants (*see* p 83). Further afield, and a sign of things to come, were two properties. The gatepiers of the former Woodburn House, now relocated at *no* 37 Woodburn Road, are good examples of gracious building in the suburbs of the town; and Eskbank House, at *no* 14 Glenesk Crescent, built by Rev James Brown, the minister for Newbattle, would become just one of many fine villas that, in the nineteenth century, would stretch out to Eskbank from the nucleus of old Dalkeith.

modern times

Dalkeith was to progress through the nineteenth and into the twentieth century as a prosperous market town **figure 15**. The Corn Exchange at *no* 200 High Street perhaps best encapsulates the standing of the burgh. Built by public subscription in 1853, it was the largest indoor grain market in Scotland **figure 16**. The establishment of banks from early in the nineteenth century is, likewise, an indication of the significant role the town played in the local economy. The Commercial Bank was built in 1810, to be followed by the National in 1825, the Royal in 1836 and the Clydesdale in 1855. These now fronted the High Street, but some older buildings remained. The tolbooth, for example, continued to act as the town gaol. The last known hanging in the street outside it was on 1 March 1827. In 1841, with the establishment of the county police and a gaol in the West Wynd, the tolbooth's role as a prison was ended.

The influx of farmers, grain merchants and other traders on market days encouraged the growth of inns and hotels. The Cross Keys Hotel, still standing, was erected by Charles, fourth duke of Buccleuch and sixth duke of Queensberry, *c* 1804. This smart hotel not only attracted the custom of those who had come to do business in the town, but also served as a stopping place for coaches and passengers on their journeys to and

figure 15
A nineteenth-century view of Dalkeith

figure 16
The Corn Exchange *c* 1853

figure 17
North Wynd
demolished *c* 1937

from the north to the Borders, and south to London. Royalty, once again, patronised the town. Dalkeith House was preferred to Holyrood by King George IV (1820–30) when he visited Scotland in 1822. Queen Victoria (1839–1901) also stayed here on a number of occasions.

In 1831, the 'innocent railway', so called because it was horse-drawn, forged closer links with the capital. It was to be mechanised in 1846, when another station was built at Eskbank on the main North British line. Closer and speedier communication with other parts of the country inevitably brought changes to all settlements; and Dalkeith was to share in this transformation. Substantial Victorian villas in the expanding suburbs and the water tower built in the 1870s to supply one of these suburbs, Eskbank, are signs of its growing role as a dormitory town to Edinburgh. Indeed, the population was sufficiently enlarged that in 1840 pressure of space was such in the old parish church that Walter, the fifth duke of Buccleuch and seventh duke of Queensberry, gifted land and endowed money for the building of the new West Church. The old parish church, often from this time called the East Church, was to undergo radical recasting and reorientation, to a design of William Burn and David Bryce, with the addition of a west gallery in 1885 and a new steeple three years later.

Much of the past was to remain until well into the twentieth century. North Wynd, for example, retained its old houses with outside staircases until 1937 **figure 17**; and it was only about this time that the extensive demolition of the east end of High Street was undertaken. In St Andrew Street, *c* 1930, the first of the town's high quality local authority schemes would replace the old closes that ran at right angles to the former Back Street. Modern developments, however, have not removed Dalkeith's historic past. There are numerous standing buildings which record previous events and circumstances (*see* pp 81–6). Most enduring, in spite of the town slowly extending into the suburbs and the forcing of a new roadway, Edinburgh Road, into the heart of the old town, is the street pattern. John Wood, who published his plan of Dalkeith in 1822 **figure 14**, Lesslie and Lawrie, both of whom produced maps of Dalkeith in the 1770s **figure 11**, and probably even those who surveyed the town for Blaeu's map in the late sixteenth or early seventeenth century **figure 9**, would have little difficulty finding their way round the town centre of Dalkeith at the end of the twentieth century.

notes

1 T Darvill, *Prehistoric Britain* (London, 1987), 63–4.
2 *Ibid*, 75.
3 *Ibid*, 103.
4 *Ibid*, 133.
5 J Barber, 'The Pit Alignment at Eskbank Nurseries', *Proceedings of the Prehistoric Society*, 51 (1985), 149–66.
6 For a fuller discussion of regional approaches to contemporary landscapes, *see* W S Hanson & D J Breeze, 'The future of Roman Scotland', in W S Hanson & E A Slater (edd), *Scottish Archaeology: New Perspectives* (Aberdeen, 1991), 72–5.
7 P Raisen & T Rees, 'Excavations of three cropmark sites at Melville Nurseries, Dalkeith', *Glas Arch Jour*, 19 (1994–5), 31–50.
8 W S Hanson & G Maxwell, *Rome's North West Frontier. The Antonine Wall* (Edinburgh, 1983), 33.
9 *Ibid*, 33–34; *cf* D J Breeze, *Roman Scotland: Frontier Country* (London, 1996) for the latest discussion.
10 *Ibid*, 39.
11 L Keppie, *Scotland's Roman Remains* (Edinburgh, 1986), 8.
12 *Ibid*, 11.
13 Hanson & Maxwell, *The Antonine Wall*, 43.
14 Keppie, *Scotland's Roman Remains*, 16.
15 *Ibid*, 18.
16 W S Hanson, *Agricola and the Conquest of the North* (London, 1987), 99.
17 G S Maxwell, *The Romans in Scotland* (Edinburgh, 1989), 71.
18 V A Maxfield, 'Excavations at Eskbank, Midlothian, 1972', *PSAS*, 105 (1972–4), 141–50.
19 Hanson, *Agricola*, 111.
20 *Ibid*, 158.
21 *Ibid*, 158.
22 *Ibid*, 158.
23 M Lynch, *Scotland: A New History* (London, 1991), 31.
24 *Ibid*, 29.
25 W F H Nicolaisen, *Scottish Place-Names: Their Study and Significance* (London, 1976).
26 J R Baldwin, *Exploring Scotland's Heritage: Lothian and the Borders* (Edinburgh, 1989), 127.
27 Nicolaisen, *Scottish Place-Names*, 71–6.
28 D Perry *et al*, 'Excavations at Castle Park, Dunbar: 1988–90' (SUAT, forthcoming); and A Smith, 'Neolithic, Bronze Age and Early Historic Features near Ratho, Edinburgh', *PSAS* 125, 115–7.
29 Nicolaisen, *Scottish Place-Names*, 73–83.
30 RCAHMS NMRS NT 36 NW 4 & 41.
31 *NSA*, vi, 451; J C Carrick, *Around Dalkeith and Camp Meg* (Leicester, 1984), 10.
32 Baldwin, *Exploring*,12; Nicolaisen, *Scottish Place-Names*, 172.
33 Cowan & Easson, *Medieval Religious Houses*, 77. The monks of Newbattle very quickly established a reputation for their wealth-creating activities. The salt-panning industry at Prestonpans, the first coal mine in Scotland, and organised agriculture in Midlothian are among the achievements accredited to them. The site of Newbattle was excavated in the 1870s and 1890s, and this revealed the massive scale of the church and monastic buildings. The inspiration for Newbattle may have been Byland Abbey in Yorkshire. The line of the monastic precinct wall may run along the east side of Newbattle Road; and there was also a deer park.
34 C Innes (ed), *Registrum de Neubotle* (Bannatyne Club, 1849), 4. *See also*, C Innes (ed), *Liber Cartarum Sancte Crucis* (Edinburgh, 1840), 9.
35 C Innes (ed), *Liber Sancte Marie de Melros* (Bannatyne Club, 1837), ii, 681, for example. J C Carrick, *Around Dalkeith* (Leicester 1984), 9. *See also*, A A M Duncan, *Scotland: The Making of The Kingdom* (Edinburgh, 1975), 562.
36 It has been argued that the castle was in existence by the reign of David II (1329–71). In all probability, however, a fortified dwelling was in Dalkeith from the twelfth century; *see* G Chalmers, *Caledonia* (Paisley, 1887), iv, 572.
37 *NSA*, vi, 498.

38 *CDS*, 183, no 355.
39 *RMS*, i, 18, no 62.
40 Quoted in Carrick, *Around Dalkeith*, 10.
41 *Ibid*, 11.
42 *RMS*, i, 117, no 335. For discussion of free forests, *see* J M Gilbert, *Hunting and Hunting Reserves in Medieval Scotland* (Edinburgh, 1979), 32–7.
43 W Fraser, *The Douglas Book* (Edinburgh, 1885), vi, 253.
44 Carrick, *Around Dalkeith*, 11.
45 *RRS*, vi, 272, no 242.
46 *RRS*, vi, 445, no 419.
47 *RRS*, vi, 458, no 435.
48 A F Stewart, *Dalkeith: Its Castle and Palace* (Edinburgh, 1925), 7.
49 *RMS*, i, 245, no 668.
50 D Laing (ed), *Registrum Domus de Soltre, necnon Ecclesie Collegiate S. Trinitas prope Edinburgh* (Bannatyne Club, 1861), 315.
51 Stewart, *Dalkeith: Its Castle and Palace*, 7.
52 T Thomson, A Macdonald & C Innes (edd), *Registrum Honoris de Morton* (Bannatyne Club, 1853), i, 151–4.
53 Cowan & Easson, 173, maintain that the year was 1396; Carrick, *Around Dalkeith*, 11, suggests the year was 1386.
54 D Ferguson, *Six Centuries In and Around the Church of St Nicholas* (Glasgow, 1951), 13.
55 *Ibid*, 13.
56 J Anderson (ed), *The Laing Charters, 854–1837* (Edinburgh, 1899), 28.
57 Ferguson, *Six Centuries*, 14.
58 A Dunlop (ed), *Calendar of Scottish Supplications to Rome, 1423–1428* (SHS, 1956), 48; Cowan & Easson, 218.
59 Cowan & Easson, 218.
60 *RMS*, ii, 592, no 2789.
61 *Ibid*, no 2789; *Laing Charters*, 176, no 679.
62 Ferguson, *Six Centuries*, 14; for information concerning the income and rental of the collegiate church at the time of the Reformation, *see* J Kirk (ed), *The Books of Assumption of the Thirds of Benefices. Scottish Ecclesiastical Rentals at the Reformation* (Oxford, 1995), 103, 110, 115–6, 141–2.
63 *RMS*, i, 334, no 840.
64 G S Pryde, *The Burghs of Scotland* (Oxford, 1965), 48.
65 *Ibid*, 58.
66 *RMS*, ii, 116, no 515.
67 *RMS*, ii, 31, no 144.
68 Little is known of this episode, and *The Scots Peerage*, ed J Balfour Paul, 9 vols (Edinburgh 1904–14), vi, 347 suggests that the lord of Dalkeith may have been party to the burning.
69 Groome, ii, 336.
70 *ER*, vi, p xxxvi.
71 R Nicholson, *Scotland: The Later Middle Ages* (Edinburgh, 1974), 364.
72 *TA*, i, 359.
73 *RMS*, ii, 62, no 273.
74 *TA*, ii, p lxviii.
75 *TA*, ii, p lxix.
76 *TA*, ii, 214.
77 *TA*, ii, 385.
78 Carrick, *Around Dalkeith*, 11–13.
79 R K Hannay (ed), *Acts of the Lords of Council in Public Affairs, 1501–1554* (Edinburgh, 1932), 147.
80 *RPC*, ii, 765; iii, 801; iv, 877; v, 815; vi, 909.
81 *RPC*, vi, 234.
82 *TA*, v, 253; *TA*, v, 258; *RMS*, iii, 352, no 1581.
83 *CSP* Scot, ii, 231.
84 *CSP* Scot, iv, 677 & 680; Groome, ii, 336.
85 *CSP* Scot, v, 358.
86 Fraser, *Douglas Book*, ii, 320.
87 *Ibid*, ii, 320.
88 *RPC*, ii, 506, 538.
89 *RPC*, iii, 580.
90 *CSP* Scot, x, 150.
91 *RPC*, iv, 596.
92 *Edin Recs 1589–1603*, 62.
93 *RPC*, v, 2.
94 *RPC*, v, 2, 507.
95 P Hume Brown (ed), *Early Travellers in Scotland* (Edinburgh, 1891), 82.
96 *CSP* Scot, x, 650.
97 *TA*, iv, 519
98 R K Hannay (ed), *Rentale Sancti Andree, 1538–1546* (SHS, 1913), p xlii.
99 J Bain (ed), *Hamilton Papers: Letters and Papers illustrating the Political Relations of England and Scotland in the Sixteenth Century* (Edinburgh, 1892), i, 398.
100 *TA*, viii, 235; 238; 242.
101 *TA*, ix, 206.

102 *CSP* Scot, 128.
103 *RSS*, iv, 130, no 763.
104 Hannay, *Acts of the Lords of Council in Public Affairs*, 603.
105 *RPC*, xiv, 170.
106 D Ferguson, *The Collegiate Church of St Nicholas* (np, 1963), 2.
107 *RSS*, vi, 335, no 1766.
108 *CSP* Scot, iv, 134.
109 *CSP* Scot, iv, 112.
110 *CSP* Scot, x, 26.
111 *TA*, v, 208.
112 *TA*, v, 211.
113 *TA*, v, 230.
114 *RPC*, xiv, 8.
115 *TA*, xi, 7.
116 *TA*, xi, 417.
117 *TA*, xii, 37.
118 *RPC*, xiv, 654.
119 *RPC*, xiv, 747.
120 *Edin Recs 1589–1603*, 194; 200.
121 *RPC*, vi, 603.
122 *RPC*, viii, 74.
123 *RPC*, viii, 345.
124 *APS*, iv, 85.
125 *NSA*, vi, 511.
126 *RPC*, v, 227.
127 *RPC*, x, 203.
128 SRO GD150/652, Morton Papers.
129 *Laing Charters*, 257, no 1040.
130 *Laing Charters*, 260, no 1489.
131 *Laing Charters*, 382, no 1578.
132 *Laing Charters*, 106, no 404.
133 *Laing Charters*, 360, no 1479.
134 *Ibid*; *RMS*, v, 49, no 157.
135 *Laing Charters*, 372, no 1536.
136 *RSS*, viii, 315, no 1876.
137 SRO, CH2/424/1, *Register of the Presbytery of Dalkeith, 1582–1630*, fo 24r.
138 *Ibid*, fo 142r.
139 SRO GD150/598, Morton Papers.
140 *RMS*, iii, 352, no 2213.
141 T Thomson (ed), *Acts of the Lords Auditors of Causes and Complaints* (London, 1839), 95.
142 *RMS*, iv, 748, no 2739.
143 W Fraser (ed), *The Lennox* (Edinburgh, 1874) ii, 454.
144 *RMS*, v, 456, no 1330.
145 *Laing Charters*, 257, no 1039; 324, no 1322, for example.
146 SRO GD150/595, Morton Papers; SRO GD150/598; for example.
147 SRO GD150/604, for example.
148 SRO GD150/599, for example.
149 *Laing Charters*, 618, no 2641, for example.
150 *Laing Charters*, 372, no 1536.
151 *Laing Charters*, 382, no 1578.
152 *Laing Charters*, 393, no 1626.
153 SRO GD150/2027, Morton Papers, Dalkeith Rental; SRO GD150/620.
154 SRO GD150/617.
155 SRO GD150/636.
156 SRO GD150/2027, Morton Papers, Dalkeith Rental; SRO GD150/613.
157 SRO GD150/615.
158 *Laing Charters*, 403, no 1666.
159 *RMS*, v, 49, no 157.
160 Groome, ii, 337.
161 *Edin Recs 1573–1589*, 265.
162 *RSS*, vii, 78, no 522.
163 J Imrie & J G Dunbar, *Accounts of the Master of Works, 1616–49* (HMSO, Edinburgh, 1982), 79, 82, 102, for example; *TA*, iv, 473.
164 *TA*, xi, 230.
165 *TA*, iv, 519.
166 *APS*, iii, 238.
167 *RMS*, v, 573, no 1674.
168 *TA*, v, 258.
169 SRO GD150/2028/1/611 Morton Papers, Dalkeith Rental. *See also* SRO, GD150/636, Morton Papers, Titles and Deeds.
170 *CSP* Scot, x, 751.
171 Hannay, *Acts of the Lords of Council*, 601.
172 Robert Smith Memorial Committee, *Robert Smith, 1722–1777, Dalkeith to Philadelphia* (Edinburgh, 1982), 15.
173 *RMS*, vi, 10, no 30.
174 SRO, CH2/424/1, Register of the Presbytery of Dalkeith, 1582–1630, fo 142r.
175 SRO GD150/2028/1/608, Morton Papers, Dalkeith Rental.
176 Ferguson, Collegiate Church, 2.
177 *Ibid*, 2.
178 *Ibid*, 2.
179 *RPC*, iv, 592.
180 *RPC*, v, 409.
181 *CSP* Scot, x, 467.
182 *RPC*, viii, 321.
183 *RPC*, viii, 460.
184 *RPC*, x, 368.
185 *RPC*, ix, 375.
186 A Macinnes, *Charles I and the Making of the Covenanting Movement* (Edinburgh, 1991), 78.

187 *RPC*, xi, 82.
188 *RPC*, xi, 115.
189 *RPC*, xi, 148, 150.
190 *RPC*, xi, p xxvi.
191 *RPC*, xii, 53.
192 Carrick, *Around Dalkeith*, 14.
193 *RPC*, Second Series, iv, 588.
194 J T Clark (ed), *MacFarlane's Genealogical Collections* (SHS, 1900), ii, 290.
195 W Fraser, *The Scotts of Buccleuch* (Edinburgh, 1878), i, p lxv.
196 Groome, ii, 336.
197 J Dickson, *The Ruined Castles of Midlothian* (Edinburgh, 1894), 56.
198 Fraser, *The Lennox*, ii, 292.
199 Fraser, *The Scotts of Buccleuch*, i, 321.
200 C Sanford Terry, *The Cromwellian Union* (SHS, 1902), pp xxv, xxvii, 3.
201 *MacFarlane's Genealogical Collections*, i, 324.
202 *Edin Recs (1642–1655)*, 318.
203 Carrick, *Around Dalkeith*, 17.
204 Fraser, *The Lennox*, i, 321.
205 *APS*, vi (2), 750.
206 *Edin Recs 1642–1655*, 48.
207 *Ibid*, 241.
208 Fraser, *The Scotts of Buccleuch*, i, 382; ii, 301.
209 T Pennant, *A Tour Of Scotland*, 3rd edition, ed B Knight (Perth, 1979), 63.
210 Carrick, *Around Dalkeith*, 18.
211 *RPC*, Third Series, ii, 714.
212 *RPC*, Third Series, iii, 744; iv, 713; v, 699; vi, 710.
213 SRO, GD 150/13/13, Morton Papers.
214 *RPC*, Third Series, vi, 268.
215 *RPC*, Third Series, ix, 184; xi, 54, 256.
216 *RPC*, Third Series, xiii, 325.
217 E W M Balfour-Melville, *An Account of the Proceedings of the Estates in Scotland, 1689–1690* (SHS, 1955), ii, 107.
218 *RPC*, xii, 707.
219 *RPC*, Second Series, i, 596.
220 *RPC*, Second Series, i, 410.
221 *RPC*, Second Series, i, 469.
222 *RPC*, Second Series, i, 624.
223 *RPC*, Second Series, iii, 142.
224 *RPC*, Second Series, iii, 385.
225 H Scott (ed), *Fasti Ecclesiae Scoticanae*, i (Edinburgh, 1915), 316.
226 *RPC*, Third Series, i, 12, 46, for example.
227 *RMS*, ix, 280.
228 *Laing Charters*, 618, no 2641.
229 *Ibid*, 648, no 1778.
230 SRO, GD150/636, Morton Papers.
231 *RPC*, xii, 710.
232 *RPC*, Second Series, iv, 129.
233 *RPC*, Second Series, v, 77.
234 *APS*, vii, 479.
235 *RPC*, Third Series, vi, 534.
236 SRO, GD150/652, Morton Papers.
237 *RMS*, ix, 445, no 1191. *See also* SRO GD 150/644, Morton Papers.
238 *RMS*, xi, 339, no 673.
239 *Laing Charters*, 170, no 653.
240 Ferguson, *Collegiate Church*, 10.
241 *RPC*, Second Series, viii, 175.
242 *RPC*, Second Series, v, 6, 331 & 355.
243 Stewart, *Dalkeith: Its Castle and Palace*, 2.
244 *RPC*, Third Series, vi, 377.
245 Ferguson, *Six Centuries*, 22.
246 *Ibid*, 22.
247 *RPC*, xi, 495.
248 All the percentages quoted are the findings of I D Whyte. These, and many of the conclusions drawn from them, are taken from I D Whyte, 'The occupational structure of Scottish burghs in the late seventeenth century', in M Lynch (ed), *The Early Modern Town in Scotland* (London, 1987), 219–44.
249 *Laing Charters*, 667, no 2866, for example.
250 G S Pryde, *Scotland from 1603 to the Present Day* (London, 1962), 33.
251 *Laing Charters*, 631, no 2072.
252 *Laing Charters*, 632, no 2706.
253 *APS*, ix, 513.
254 *RPC*, Third Series, viii, 115.
255 D Defoe, *A Tour Through the Whole Island of Great Britain, 1724*, ed P N Furbank & W R Owens (Newhaven, 1991), 341.
256 SRO, GD 224/213/3, Buccleuch Muniments, Account Books.
257 *Robert Smith*, 11.
258 SRO, GD 224/213/3, Buccleuch Muniments, Account Books.
259 *Robert Smith*, 12.
260 Kilmarnock District Council, MS 1/1/1.
261 J A Mackay, *The History of the Burgh of Kilmarnock and of Loudon District* (Kilmarnock, 1992), 48.

262 D W Kemp (ed), *Pococke's Tours in Scotland, 1747, 1750, 1760* (SHS, 1887), 312.
263 *OSA*, ii, 214.
264 *Robert Smith*, 10.
265 Defoe, *Tour*, 341.
266 *OSA*, ii, 212.
267 *Ibid*, ii, 212.
268 R Heron (ed), *Scotland Delineated* (Edinburgh, 1975), 372.
269 SRO, B52/3/3, 3 March 1764.
270 J Paterson, *History of the Regality of Musselburgh* (Musselburgh, 1861), 54.
271 SRO, B52/3/3, 30 Sept. 1728.
272 *Ibid*, 5 Nov. 1716.
273 *RCRB*, iv, 381.
274 *RCRB*, iv, 162.
275 *RCRB*, iv, 211, 333.
276 *RCRB*, iv, 513.
277 *Laing Charters*, 705, no 3058.
278 *Laing Charters*, 710, no 3081.
279 *OSA*, ii, 213.
280 *Ibid*, ii, 213.
281 J Gray (ed), *Scottish Population Statistics* (SHS, 1952), 15; cf I D Whyte, 'Urbanization in early-modern Scotland: a preliminary analysis', *Scottish Economic and Social History*, ix (1989), 25.
282 Defoe, *Tour*, 341.
283 Heron (ed), *Scotland Delineated*, 372.
284 SRO, GD 224/212/2/16; GD 224/214/2, Buccleuch Muniments, Account Books.
285 Ferguson, *Collegiate Church*, 2.
286 Ferguson, *Six Centuries*, 20.
287 *OSA*, ii, 217.
288 Fraser, *Scotts of Buccleuch*, i, 476.
289 E P Dennison & R Coleman, *Historic Musselburgh: the Archaeological Implications of Development* (Scottish Burgh Survey, 1996), 32.
290 Fraser, *Scotts of Buccleuch*, 326.
291 *OSA*, ii, 215.
292 *Robert Smith*, 12.
293 *OSA*, ii, 215.
294 *OSA*, ii, 214.
295 SRO, GD 224/214/2, Buccleuch Muniments, Account Books.
296 *Robert Smith*, 12.
297 *Robert Smith*, 14.
298 Ferguson, *Collegiate Church*, 2.
299 C Rogers, *Social Life in Scotland* (Grampian Club, 1886), 79.
300 *OSA*, ii, 215.
301 SRO, GD 224/212/2/23, Buccleuch Muniments, Account Books.
302 SRO, GD 224/212/2/24, Buccleuch Muniments, Account Books.
303 SRO, GD 224/214/2, Buccleuch Muniments, Account Books.
304 SRO, GD 224/232/11, Buccleuch Muniments, Account Books.
305 SRO, GD 224/208/1/35–52, Buccleuch Muniments, Account Books.
306 *Ibid.*
307 *Robert Smith*, 12.
308 W B Blaikie (ed), *Itinerary of Prince Charles Edward Stewart* (SHS, 1897), 23–4.
309 SRO, GD 224/214/2, Buccleuch Muniments, Account Books.
310 SRO, GD 224/207/1, Buccleuch Muniments, Account Books.

area by area assessment

pp 49–57

D

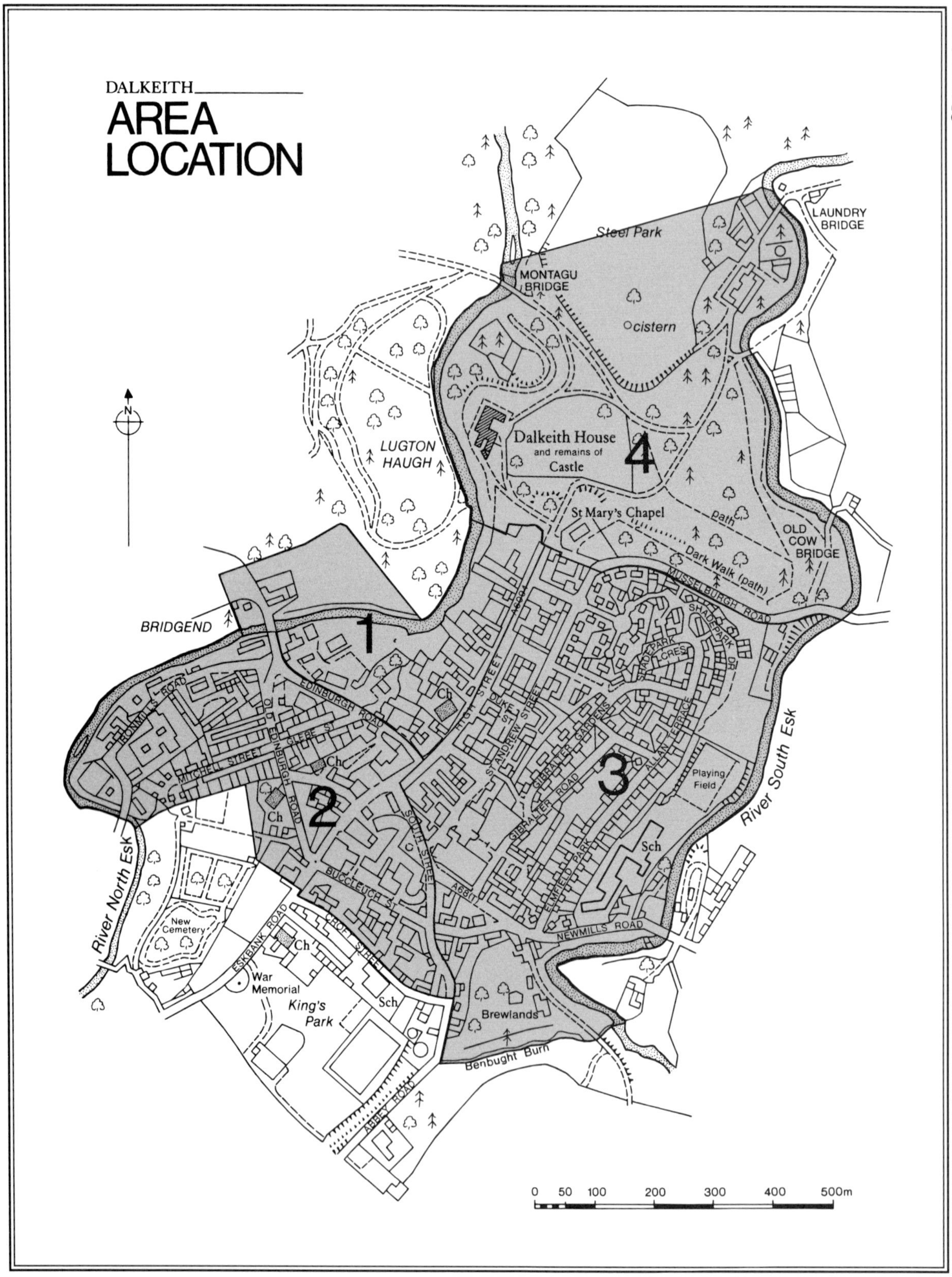

Area location map

introduction

Dalkeith has been divided into four areas for ease of reference **figure 18**. The area under study extends beyond the historic core of the town to incorporate Dalkeith House (which is also the site of the palace and early castle) and its grounds, the bridges over the Rivers North and South Esk, the numerous mills which were sited along the south bank of the River North Esk, and outlying fields such as the glebe and brewlands. Medieval Dalkeith probably stretched over a section of the land now incorporated in Dalkeith Parks (*see* p 30). The boundaries for this study are formed by both natural and artificial features. The rivers form natural northern and southern boundaries and largely contained the development of the medieval town. The eastern and western limits are more arbitrary in their definition, with the eastern boundary cutting across Steel Park. To the west, the boundary follows Croft Street before cutting across to the River South Esk.

As the High Street forms the central division between Area 1 to the north and Area 3 to the south, both areas overlap a little to take in the frontage on the opposite side of the street. This ensures that important features of the medieval townscape, such as the market place, which occupied the width of the street, and the market cross which was situated in the middle of the street, are not overlooked. Similarly, Areas 1 and 2 overlap slightly as the division between these two lies in the middle of Edinburgh Road.

area 1

High Street/Dalkeith House grounds/River North Esk/Bridgend/Edinburgh Road **figure 19**

description

The section of High Street contained within Area 1 comprises a mixture of the old and the new, with St Nicholas Church **figure 10.A** at one end of the spectrum, the oldest extant feature of medieval Dalkeith, and, at the other, modern sheltered housing developments. The church dominates the townscape, as it has for centuries, both in its size and siting, jutting as it now does into the street. At the west end of this area is Edinburgh Road, a late addition to the town plan. Nearby is Brunton's Close **B**, a narrow close with newly renovated buildings, one of the few reminders of the narrowness of the numerous vennels that led off the High Street in former times. At the east end of this area are the Duke's Gates **C**, the west entrance to Dalkeith House, a clear reminder of Dalkeith's origins as a settlement dependent on a fortified residence. With the main traffic now diverted across the west end of the High Street, down South Street, the eastern end, leading to Musselburgh Road, is quiet by comparison, and its considerable width adds to the illusion of emptiness.

The High Street lies on a fairly narrow ridge, from which the ground falls steeply down to the River North Esk **figures 2** *&* **3**. This is best demonstrated at the graveyard of St Nicholas Church, where the boundary wall sits on the very edge of the ridge. Immediately adjacent to the graveyard, on the north-west side, is one of the few empty spaces left on either side of the High Street, an overgrown garden **D**. Elsewhere along the High Street, there is a mixture of modern dwellings, mostly sheltered housing, with some private villas at the east end, near the grand entrance to Dalkeith House. Some commercial properties front onto the street but most sit further back, behind the main frontage.

At the bottom of the steep slope, along the south bank of the North Esk, is Grannies Park **E**. This was one of the industrial zones of the town and to a certain extent is still, with former mill buildings having been converted for commercial use. The Lugton Bridge **F**, close to the site of the original bridge crossing, still carries the main traffic in and out of Dalkeith. A small settlement developed at the northern approach to the bridge, on either side of the road, close to where the present houses stand today.

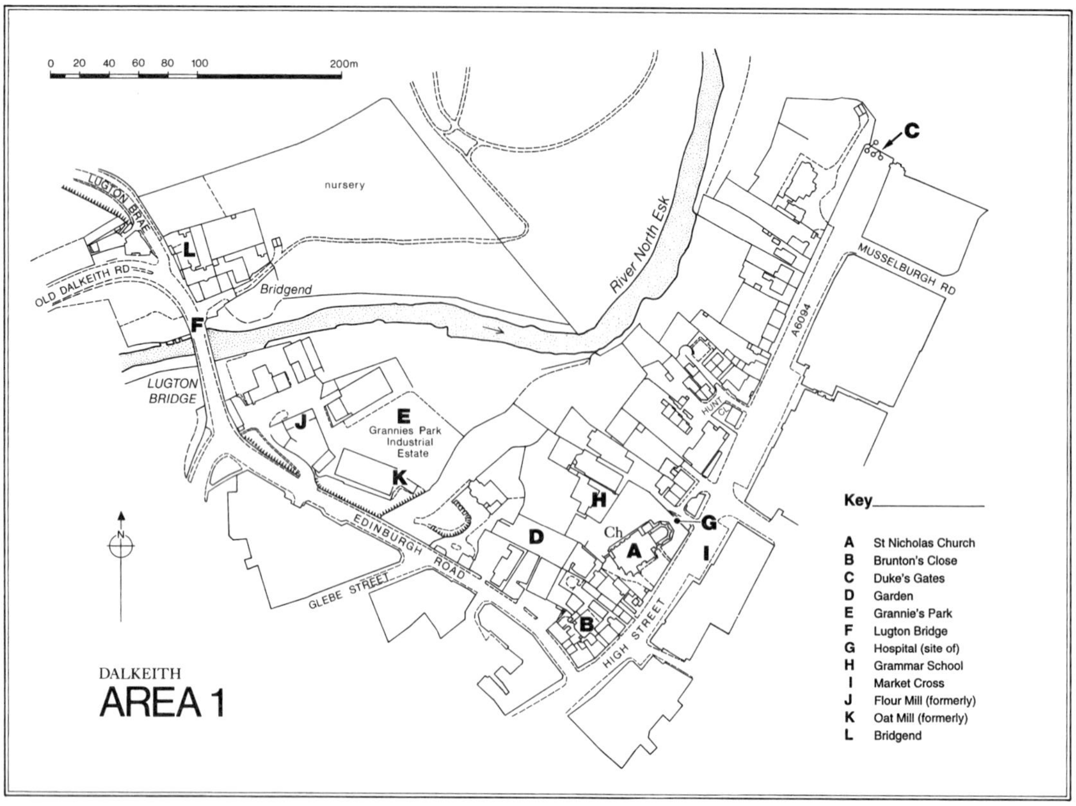

figure 19
Area 1

historical background

St Nicholas Church and related buildings

St Nicholas Church **A** dominates this area. In 1369/1370, a chantry was founded in the chapel of Dalkeith, although whether this means that a chapel stood in the little township or was established within the nearby castle is unclear. There was certainly a chapel in the township in the later fourteenth century, but its exact date of foundation is not known. It might have been established as early as 1372, if not earlier, when consent was given to found a chaplainry in the chapel of St Nicholas, which stood in the town. The fact that the chapel of St Nicholas was undergoing repairs to its roof, at a cost of £20, in 1390 is firm indication of its existence at least by this date (*see* pp 19–20).

In 1405, a provost and five chaplains were endowed by Sir James (Douglas) on the chapel of St Nicholas, raising it to the status of a collegiate church. It may have undergone some rebuilding around 1420. It is known that one of the altars, which may

archaeological potential and future development

The most recent Dalkeith Local Plan (1980) is now out of date, and many of the planning proposals contained within it have already been implemented. It does, however, state that there are few edge-of-town sites suitable for office or housing developments and that gap sites within the town would be utilised. Grannies Park **E** has been earmarked for environmental improvements, but so far little has been done. This is an area with a long industrial history and should also be treated as sensitive for its industrial archaeology.

Area 1 lies at the core of the medieval town and its archaeological potential is, therefore, very high. Contained within Area 1 are a wide range of important sites and features, including the market place, a section of the main street frontage, burgage plots, the earliest church and the site of the hospital. On the fringes of the area were a number of mills and a lade, outlying fields and a small settlement by the Lugton Bridge. Due to the lack of any previous archaeological work in Dalkeith, and in the absence of any chance finds from the historic core, only general comments can be made at present about the archaeological potential of Dalkeith.

have stood in the choir, was dedicated to the Blessed Virgin, as a charter was signed at it in 1432. By 1467 the collegiate church was to become, also, the parish church of Dalkeith, as opposed to being subordinate to the parish church of Lasswade. In 1475 and 1477, the college was expanded by James Douglas, the first earl of Morton, whose tomb, along with that of his wife, Joanna, daughter of King James I (1406–37), lies in the choir **figure 7**; and in 1503 two further chaplainries were established, dedicated to the Holy Rood and St John the Baptist, the latter situated in the south aisle. References in 1504 and 1557 to a chaplainry dedicated to the Crucifix may be indication of a new endowment, although this may simply be the chaplainry of the Holy Rood under another name. There were also, apparently, two further altars, that dedicated to St Peter, which stood in the north transept, and that dedicated to St Nicholas, which was in the centre of the chancel.

St Nicholas Church was to undergo change after the Reformation. The choir was sealed off and abandoned in 1590 as a 'monument of idolatry'; although the collegiate church still had a provost in 1593. The western part continued to function as the parish church **figure 10**. In 1591, it was in a poor material state, although the congregation and minister declared themselves willing to repair it. In 1594, a platform was built on the steeple, its main purpose being to 'bear ane brassen piece', but whether this is a reference to a cannon or extra roofing is unclear. It is unlikely to have been a decorative addition, unless it is associated with the bells which are known to have been in use. Major transformation work was undertaken in the interior, including the insertion of some lofts, or seats, for the incorporated crafts.

Dalkeith was caught up in both religious and political upheaval in the seventeenth century (*see* pp 27–33), which inevitably had an effect on St Nicholas Church. In 1622, the congregation was swelled, like those of Tranent and Duddingston, by Edinburgh parishioners who objected to kneeling at communion. The parish church, as many others, was used by the leader of the Independents, Oliver Cromwell, as a military barracks and stable for his horses, after the defeat of the Scots at Dunbar on 3 September 1650. General Monck was resident in the town for a number of years; and it was here, in the churchyard, that he buried one of his children in February 1657. The death of Mary, countess of Buccleuch, followed four years later; her remains were placed in the Buccleuch burial vault (*see* p 29).

In 1660, after the misuse of the Cromwellian period and natural deterioration, the parish church was made wind- and water-tight. Since the turn of the century the interior had housed some lofts of the local craftsmen (*see* p 27). A loft for the Earl of Buccleuch had been erected in 1645; and from 1660 there was a rapid escalation in the construction of lofts. At the west end of the church were the lofts of the baxters, fleshers, dyers, weavers and the common lofts; to the north the tailors' loft; to the north-west, the

history

---

archaeology

The partly ruinous collegiate church of St Nicholas **figure 10** *&* **A**, constructed sometime in the mid to late fourteenth century, is the oldest surviving feature of medieval Dalkeith. The choir, the only part to escape restoration in the mid nineteenth century but now becoming increasingly ruinous, is protected as a Scheduled Ancient Monument. Extensions, alterations and restorations over the centuries mean structural elements of earlier phases of the church, including the original chapel, may be preserved within the present building. Indeed, parts of the south porch and the piers in the nave survive from the medieval church. Other elements may also have been incorporated into the fabric itself, or may equally survive as foundations sealed below the present floor levels. The position of the church is interesting as it stands slightly skewed in relation to the present alignment of the High Street, and its graveyard almost seems to 'jut out' into the street. Kirkyard boundaries often change, due to encroachment for secular use, and it is quite possible that medieval burials might be found beneath the present street.

Beside the church was a hospital **G**, designated a *maison dieu*, founded in 1386, or possibly 1396, by Sir James Douglas. Nothing remains of it today and its exact location is not clear. The archaeological remains of this hospital might be preserved below standing merchants and skinners; and to the south the hammermen. The shoemakers had their loft below that of the merchants and the scholars beneath the tailors. The last loft to be constructed was that for the colliers, erected in the chancel in 1838. All were demolished during the huge renovations that were undertaken in 1851, but their previous existence remains an interesting comment on the range of crafts in seventeenth- and eighteenth-century Dalkeith. In spite of this seventeenth-century upgrading, there is evidence, in 1675, that the sacristy of St Nicholas Church was functioning as a prison, perhaps because of building works at the tolbooth, the traditional prison, at this time.

Eighteenth-century records indicate that the parish church was often under repair. The clock in the steeple, for example, was cleaned in 1724; and the main spring needed repair work four years later. By 1752, however, the steeple was in a ruinous state and so dangerous that it had to be taken down. For its own safety the congregation was obliged to worship in a field. Ten years later, a new steeple was erected and the old bells were replaced, all at a cost of £540 19s 8¾d. Due to neglect, the roof of the old church, blocked off from the body of the church since the sixteenth century (*see* p 51), fell in.

In 1841, with the growth in the number of parishioners, an overflow church, the West Church, was built on Old Edinburgh Road; thereafter many would call the old parish church of St Nicholas the 'East Church'. The East Church underwent radical recasting and reorientation in 1851–5, to the design of William Burn and David Bryce; it had a west gallery added in 1885 and a new steeple in 1888.

Closely associated with the church in the middle ages was the hospice or hospital G, also founded in the late fourteenth century (*see* p 20) and still functioning after the Reformation. A charity workhouse was later set up, which could house up to forty inmates. John Wood's plan of 1822 **figure 14** sites this immediately to the west of St Nicholas Church. According to Lesslie's plan of *c* 1770 **figure 11**, there was also a poor house, which stood on the east side of the Old Edinburgh Road, north of the glebe, near to the Lugton Bridge. This was erected in 1747 by the Kirk Session.

A school was probably attached to the church throughout the middle ages. By 1584, there was more than one school in the town as, in this year, John Ker was gifted the altarage of St John the Baptist, for the support he had given to 'the sculeis' over the previous seven years. Moreover, Mr Andrew Alane was a schoolmaster in Dalkeith in 1582, which also suggests more than one schoolmaster. In 1591, it was decided that, for the duration of Mr George Hastie's time in Dalkeith, there should be only one school and that

history

archaeology

buildings around the church. Little is known about the form of such early urban hospitals but this one is likely to have been a small complex, perhaps a single building, as it was originally built for only six poor people.

Buildings situated in the core of the medieval burgh were almost certainly constructed on the site of, or directly over the remains of, earlier buildings, a sequence possibly going back to the medieval period and continuing up to the present day. Although there has been no opportunity to examine, archaeologically, any of the street frontages in Dalkeith, evidence of earlier, possibly medieval, structures may be expected to survive, sealed beneath eighteenth- or nineteenth-century standing buildings along the High Street and the vennels leading off it.

In other Scottish towns, archaeological excavations have revealed that street frontages have potential for the preservation of archaeological deposits, in spite of the fact that cellarage may have destroyed earlier evidence. Recent excavations in Perth, Dunfermline and Arbroath have also shown that the width and alignment of the main streets in the burghs have changed over the centuries. Earlier cobbled street surfaces and contemporary buildings may therefore be preserved up to three or four metres behind the line of the modern street frontage. At 80–86 High Street, Perth, for instance, the medieval street lay some four metres further back from the present High Street. At the Abbot House, in Dunfermline, recent excavations uncovered a whole section of the medieval street itself, inside and sealed below the floor of the standing building; up to six phases of street the 'bairnes' should be encouraged to return to it, which implies that rivalry between schools and absenteeism had arisen. From 1622 to 1647, however, it was reported that there was no functioning school in the town, due to lack of funds. Following the 1646 Founding of Schools Act, the Earl of Buccleuch opened a new school, probably the same one noted in the privy council records in 1680 as taking in boarders.

It is known that by the eighteenth century, on what was probably the original site of the old school, the grammar school **H**, as well as the master's house, was located behind the parish church. For much of the eighteenth century it was one of the most celebrated in the country. Attended by all classes of society, including children of aristocrats and local gentry, its pupils included John Adam, the son of architect William Adam; Robert Smith from Lugton, who was to become a famous architect in Philadelphia; probably John Kay, the engraver; and many others. In 1729, repair work was being undertaken on the building, at the expense of the Buccleuchs. In 1741, the rector, John Love, had recommended that the school roof should be re-thatched or slated, thus indicating that the school was thatched—as, indeed, many of the houses would have been at this time. The school was in need of tables and forms as well as windows in 1752; but in 1774, it was reported by Lord President Forbes to his sister that the school was 'in very good order and the boys well taken care of. The whole expense for a year, including the masters fees and cloaths, [did] not exceed £25'. For a while its reputation declined, but due to the diligence of rectors in the last decades of the century, its fame was somewhat restored. About twenty of the scholars boarded with the rector in the 1790s. By this time, there were also four English schools in the town, all of which were apparently well attended, one attracting as many as eighty to a hundred pupils.

the market place, markets and fairs

The street in front of St Nicholas Church and extending eastwards is wide. This is because it functioned as the important market place for Dalkeith, and it was here that the market cross stood **I**. In 1401, Robert III (1390–1406) granted to Sir James Douglas of Dalkeith that his 'villa' should be held as a free burgh of barony. (In 1540, it was elevated to the status of a burgh of regality.) Presumably having the right to hold a market, one of the basic rights of burghs, the town would have attracted traders from the surrounding rural hinterland. Increased trade meant increased prosperity, not only for the burgh superior, but

history

archaeology

surfaces were revealed, each separated by thick dumps of midden containing broken pottery, leather and oyster shells. Here, archaeology has demonstrated clearly how dramatically street frontages can shift over time, and has highlighted the potential for archaeological deposits to be buried below later buildings.

The potential for medieval archaeological levels, particularly earlier buildings, to be preserved beneath present-day standing buildings in this area of Dalkeith is likely to be concentrated along High Street.

A double circle of stones **I**, near the centre of the High Street, marks the site of the old market cross of Dalkeith. This is a useful reminder that the High Street itself was the centre of activity and its archaeological potential should not be forgotten when considering, for example, environmental improvements, the insertion of new services or the renewal of old services. Evidence of medieval street levels may be preserved, either as metalled surfaces or as accumulated midden deposits (as at Abbot House, Dunfermline). The remains of other important features of the medieval townscape may also be sealed beneath the present road surface—the market cross, ports and wells—of which no archaeological evidence has yet been found. Similarly, the smaller wynds should also be monitored routinely.

Behind the High Street frontage were the backlands of the burgage plots. Over time, these were gradually built over as pressure for space within the town increased—a process known as repletion. Evidence of burgage plots can survive, buried beneath modern for the town itself as well. Some of the grain sold at the weekly corn market, held on a Sunday until 1581, when it was transferred to a Tuesday, was grown by the burgesses on land around the burgh. Without doubt, by this time Dalkeith was functioning as a market centre for many rural settlements in the vicinity.

Other markets were, clearly, still held on a Sunday, as in 1583 the Edinburgh magistrates enacted that none of their burgesses should attend any Sunday markets in neighbouring towns, including Dalkeith. The markets were not only for the sale and purchase of victuals. The local craftsmen, such as the cutler, John Lytoun, an indweller in the town in 1576, the wrights who were also employed on the crown's business, the coopers and the smiths would also sell their products. The town obviously had numerous baxters, brewers, fleshers and cadgers, necessary not only to supply the palace, but also the national army and troops so often billeted in the town in the sixteenth to eighteenth centuries (*see* pp 21–39). The town also had the right to hold a fair. This would attract merchants from much further afield in Scotland, and from abroad. From 1581, its appointed date was 10 October.

Fairs and weekly markets continued throughout the seventeenth century in spite of the upheaval of billeted troops and the like. Occasional crises, such as plague in Preston and Prestonpans, meant that the markets and fairs of Dalkeith, along with those of Haddington, Preston and Tranent, were banned for some six weeks in 1636. Such setbacks did not prevent the emergence of Dalkeith as an important market. Neither is it surprising that there should have been so many grain mills and ancillary buildings in the town (*see* pp 23, 35 *&* 56). Apart from the obvious natural geographical advantage of a superb water supply, it was said of Dalkeith, in 1724, that it was a 'pretty large market-town, and the better market for being so near to Edinburgh; for there comes great quantities of provisions here from the southern countries, which are brought up here to be carried to Edinburgh market again, and sold there'. One of the most important commodities brought to Dalkeith was grain. Indeed, it was said that Dalkeith was 'perhaps the greatest grain market in Scotland'; and that this grain, once sold, brought 'ready' money, which the farmers then spent in the town. Some of the grain was transported to the west, to supply such towns as Carron, Glasgow and Paisley. Clearly this weekly market, held on a Thursday, functioned as an important distribution point not only for the capital. As well as this Thursday market, there was also a meal market, held every Monday from Martinmas to Whitsun.

history

archaeology

buildings and car parks. Burgage plots are an extremely valuable source of information to the urban historian and archaeologist as they often document the activities and conditions of everyday life in a medieval town. Excavations in other medieval towns in Scotland, such as Perth, Aberdeen and St Andrews, have revealed middens, rubbish pits, cess pits and vegetable plots as common features of medieval backlands, alongside craft workshops and kilns. A series of three excavations at Canal Street, in Perth, for example, showed that the boundaries of these plots appear to have been shifted regularly, revealing a fascinating sequence of continually changing plot boundaries, reflecting the amalgamation and sub-division of properties throughout the medieval period.

The end of the burgage plots was sometimes marked by small walls, wooden fences or ditches, beyond which may have been a back lane, although the topography of this part of Dalkeith suggests that this is unlikely north of High Street. This is best illustrated in the graveyard of St Nicholas Church where the ground falls away sharply down to Grannies Park **E** and the River North Esk, suggesting that the plots on this side of the High Street must have been fairly short. On the opposite side of the High Street, the plots may have been considerably longer. As is the case in most medieval towns, the backlands of Dalkeith's early burgage plots have been built over, but any further developments here should be archaeologically monitored as remnants of the burgage plots themselves, their boundaries and the activities which took place within them, may be preserved below ground.

Dalkeith's role as a grain market was reinforced by its weekly cattle market, held every Tuesday. This brought not merely stock farmers to the town with money to spend, but also provided the town's butchers with the necessary animals to supply the Edinburgh market. On some occasions, it was said, the consumers in the capital took all the meat the Dalkeith butchers could kill. The local craftsmen also took some advantage of the by-products of the butchers' activities (*see* p 34). As well as this weekly market, the town also held an annual fair on the third Tuesday of October. This catered largely for the trade in horses and black cattle.

The Corn Exchange **figure 16** (*see* **area 3**), built in the mid nineteenth century, although now somewhat dilapidated, epitomises Dalkeith's function as an important market town. Built by public subscription, it was the largest indoor grain market in Scotland.

High Street and the townscape

Dalkeith town was, for much of its history, essentially one street, called the High Street, running approximately east to west, away from the castle. By 1430, and probably of very much earlier date, this main street, originally called 'the great road', was established and lined with burgage plots. A number of vennels or wynds ran from the High Street. Lining the street were the tenements and burgage plots of the burgesses. It is interesting that these plots were commonly called 'cottage lands', 'cotlands,' 'cottage tenements', 'husbandlands' or 'husband tenements', rather than tofts, rigs or burgage plots, as is the norm in burghs of this period. This is probably a reflection of the predominantly agricultural nature of the town.

There is no evidence that the town was encircled with walls, although many medieval Scottish towns surrounded themselves with ditches and palisading. It is quite probable that this was also the case in Dalkeith, perhaps at the foot of the burgage plots. The tofts in this part of the town may not have been so delineated, since many of them terminate at the North Esk. The river would provide at least a psychological, if not a highly defensible physical barrier. Entrance to and exit from the town would have been either through small gates at the back of the burgage plots or through the main gates, or ports, of the town. Closes running back from the High Street, on both sides, were now developed with dwellings and workshops. Brunton's Close **B** by 115/117 High Street still retains many of its original characteristics and gives an insight into eighteenth-century Dalkeith. Visitors to

history

archaeology

Several changes have been made to the town plan in the last 200 years or so to aid access into the town and to provide extra housing, but these modern developments may conceal earlier medieval features. The Edinburgh Road is a late insertion into the town plan, dating from the late eighteenth or early nineteenth century. It provides the most direct route into town from the Lugton Bridge, and Lesslie's *c* 1770 map of the town **figure 11** indicates that some earlier buildings may have been demolished to make way for it. Their foundations may be preserved below ground. Brunton's Close **B** is also a later insertion, this time of the eighteenth century, and was built over a former enclosed garden.

A small settlement, Bridgend **L**, is known to have existed on the north bank of the River North Esk, adjacent to Lugton Bridge. Lesslie's map shows a small clustering of approximately seven buildings on either side of the approach road to the bridge (Old Edinburgh Road), some of which still stand today. Later buildings here may incorporate elements of earlier buildings in their fabric. The bridge itself dates to 1765, but was remodelled in 1816 to carry increased traffic. An earlier bridge lay a short distance down river; although its exact location is uncertain, its foundations may still survive on the river banks.

Lesslie's and Wood's maps **figures 11 *&* 14** both show a number of industrial sites in Dalkeith, some within Area 1. The industries represented were common to the medieval period and may have been long established. Many industries required regular supplies of water, or indeed used water as a source of power. Mills are recorded as early as 1540 in

Dalkeith commented favourably on the townscape. Daniel Defoe wrote in 1724 that the 'town [was] spacious, and well built, and [was] the better, no doubt, for the neighbourhood of so many noblemen's and gentlemen's houses of such eminence in the neighbourhood'. By the end of the century it was said of the town that it was 'though not a royal borough ... a considerable place ... it contain[ed] one very handsome street, beside lanes'. Eighteenth-century maps **figure 11** also suggest that the increase in population had little effect on the street pattern. In any town, the street lay-out is the most enduring topographical feature. The main street was by now fully built up, and there is cartographic evidence of repletion, or building in the backlands. This was more marked on the south side of the street than on the north, partly due to the fact that the land behind the street frontage on the north fell steeply down to the Esk.

mills

The plan of Dalkeith, drawn by John Lesslie *c* 1770, indicates the importance of mills in the town **figure 11**. Both the North Esk and the South Esk provided water power. In Lesslie's plan, a flour mill **J** and oat mill **K** are depicted drawing water from the North Esk. The flour mill can still be seen in Grannies Park. An L-shaped building of three storeys and a loft, its attached cartshed is a little later; but the arched mill race depicted on the map is still visible. Re-use of mill buildings was commonplace; there are remnants of a skinnery at Grannies Park; and an old kiln was removed only this century. Mills had been an important part of Dalkeith's economy since the middle ages. The town had more than one mill by 1540, one being called the Pow Mill. At least one of these mills was supplied by water controlled by the 'water yett' that stood on the Hauch of Dalkeith, by a little oak tree, on the way to Braehead. On 1 December 1583, it is recorded that the rentals of the corn mills of Dalkeith were £200, a not insignificant sum; and by 1587, there were four grain and cloth mills in Dalkeith.

communications

history

Close to the mills stands Lugton Bridge **F**, very near to the sites of the original medieval bridge and fording point, which were a little down-river. Situated as Dalkeith was between

archaeology

Dalkeith, and the River North Esk was no doubt the most attractive location for them. The sweeping bend in the river here allowed water to be drawn off to power the mills and to be returned to the river downstream. Over the years, many mills were converted from one specific use to another as the economy dictated. The two mills in this area depicted on Lesslie's map, a flour mill **J** and oat mill **K**, may have been built over, or incorporated, earlier mills. Rather little is known about the form of medieval mills in Scotland, as few have been excavated. Their archaeological potential is demonstrated, however, by an excavation at Saracen Head Inn, Glasgow, where the remains of a flour mill were found three metres below the present ground surface. A timber-lined channel drew water from the old Poldrait Burn to power a vertical mill wheel, an impression of which survived in the stream bed; one of the paddles and a stone socket for the axle were also found in the stream. The mill itself was timber-built with a porched loading bay for carts.

two branches of the Esk, its bridges were an important feature of the townscape. The importance of maintenance of adequate modes of communication with neighbouring burghs and, in particular, with Edinburgh is highlighted by the concern for maintenance of roads and bridges. An act of parliament of 1594, for example, specifically dealt with the issue of mending and maintaining the two bridges at Dalkeith, the north one over the North Esk (Lugton Bridge) and the south one over the South Esk (Cow Bridge), which were 'now almaist decayed'.

The necessity for ready access was summed up in 1614, when a licence was given to the community and inhabitants of Dalkeith 'to uplift a tax for the repairing of bridges north and south of the town which [were] in danger of being carried away by the ice and snow from the heights, which will be of great inconvenience in respect of the great traffic over them to Edinburgh, and from the same to all parts of the realm lately called the Borders'. Carts were to pay two pence Scots and horses that were led, one penny. Interestingly, and unusually, this toll had to be paid not only on crossing the bridges, but also if traversing the rivers by the nearest fords to the bridges. Tolls from those using either the bridge or ford (unspecified) were, again, instituted in 1631. Two years later, the shire commissioners were requested to ride the road from Dalkeith to Edinburgh to consider where they felt it should be enlarged or repaired, such was the importance of the thoroughfare. In 1663, parliament recognised the strategic importance of these two crossings over the Esk, both for locals and strangers, as this was the main route from the south of the kingdom to Edinburgh. Permission was given for tolls to be raised for fifteen years to facilitate repair, since the bridges had been almost undermined by 'great inundations of water' in 1659 and since that time they were 'daylie decaying and [would] shortly fall to the ground'. It is clear that the commodities whose weight caused most damage were to be targeted: millstones, cart loads, horse loads of coal, lime, victual and ale, and sheep, cattle and horses en route to market. By 1680, it is recorded that the Dalkeith–Edinburgh route was once again in disrepair.

Public buildings, bridges and roadways were a constant drain on town finances, even though much was financed by the Dukes of Buccleuch. In September 1725, for example, part of the highway near Bridgend **L** was under repair; and a month later a hole in Lugton Bridge had to be patched. Maintenance of this important crossing point was to be a priority for the town well into the twentieth century.

history

archaeology

Where there are mills there are also weirs, leats (lades) and mill races. A weir was required to divert water from a river or stream to a channel, or leat. A 'tail race' returned the water that had been through the mill to the river, to prevent 'back-water' impeding the mill-wheel. The tail race of a mill was found at Balfarg, Fife. An extensive network of leats and tail-races can be seen on Lesslie's map, all of which have since disappeared except for the arch over the mill race. The mills, however, have survived (*see* p 84) and any development within the present standing buildings may reveal whether their origins pre-date the eighteenth century. The leats and tail races have been backfilled but are likely to be preserved below the present ground surface. Environmental improvements are envisaged for Grannies Park **E**, which is now largely commercial land; any future developments here should be monitored archaeologically as a matter of routine.

GD03032G/1998
DALKEITH
AREA 2
N
River North Esk
LUGTON BRIDGE
IRONMILLS ROAD
ESKVIEW GROVE
EDINBURGH ROAD
OLD EDINBURGH ROAD
GLEBE STREET
MITCHELL STREET
NORTH WYND
HIGH STREET
SOUTH STREET
IRONMILLS ROAD
IRONMILLS PARK
Indoor Bowling Stadium
ESKBANK ROAD
BUCCLEUCH STREET
CROFT STREET
LOTHIAN ST
LONDON RD
LOTHIAN ROAD
CROFT ST
Key
A 'Town Centre'
B Midlothian Council Headquarters
C Stables
D Site of Glebe
E West Church
F Watch Tower
G Scottish Examination Board
H? Poor House (site of)
I Barley Mill (site of)
J Waulk Mill
M Cattle Market (site of)
0 20 40 60 80 100 200m

figure 20

Area 2

area 2

Edinburgh Road/High Street/South Street/Croft Street/Mitchell Street/River North Esk **figure 20**

description

This part of Dalkeith has experienced the most development pressures, but the former street pattern has been largely reinstated in the modern town plan. Three blocks of buildings, known as the 'Town Centre' **A**, comprise shops with flats and offices above. The pedestrianised courts reinstate the former vennels: The Wicket, White Hart Street and West Wynd.

This is easily the busiest part of town; traffic management is, and always seems to have been, a problem. There are a number of new developments in this area, not least Midlothian Council's headquarters on Buccleuch Street **B**. To the south-west of Buccleuch Street lies Croft Street. The properties on the north side of the street here have recently been renovated as part of a new housing association development. An interesting block of stables **C** lay at the corner of Croft Street and Lothian Road, but was in a state of disrepair in 1995.

The north end of Area 2 maps the gradual expansion of the town. Glebe Street was developed in the nineteenth century over what had still been open fields at the end of the previous century **D**. The West Church **E**, constructed in 1840 to house the overflowing congregation of St Nicholas, stands on the west side of the Old Edinburgh Road. Closed in 1989, it is now used as a cabinet maker's workshop. The New Burial Ground (1827) lies on the opposite side of the road, and contains the octagonal Watch Tower **F**, built to accommodate armed watchmen to deter graverobbers. Further down the slope, towards the North Esk, the developments become progressively more modern, culminating in the Scottish Examination Board's black glass headquarters on Ironmills Road **G**.

historical background

High Street and the townscape

Dalkeith town was, for much of its history, essentially one street, called the High Street, running approximately east to west, away from the castle. By 1430, and probably of very much earlier date, this main street, originally called 'the great road', was established and lined with burgage plots. A number of vennels or wynds ran from the High Street. Lining the street were the tenements and burgage plots of the burgesses. It is interesting that these plots were commonly called 'cottage lands', 'cotlands,' 'cottage tenements', 'husbandlands' or 'husband tenements', rather than tofts, rigs or burgage plots, as is the norm in burghs of this period. This is probably a reflection of the predominantly agricultural nature of the town.

archaeological potential and future development

The most recent Dalkeith Local Plan (1980) is now largely out of date, and many of the planning proposals contained within it have already been implemented. It states that a few edge-of-town sites are suitable for office or housing developments and that gap sites within the town would be utilised. The south bank of the River North Esk, along Ironmills Road, has seen considerable development in recent years, both for housing and commercial use. This area should also be treated as sensitive for its industrial archaeological interest.

Much of Area 2 lay on the fringes of the medieval town, and has since borne the brunt of nineteenth-century expansion and traffic management measures. Contained within Area 2, however, are a wide range of sites and features including a section of the main street frontage, vennels and burgage plots and the new parish church. Mills were sited along the southern bank of the River North Esk and also leased outlying fields. Settlement

There is no evidence that the town was encircled with walls, although many medieval Scottish towns surrounded themselves with ditches and palisading. It is quite probable that this was also the case in Dalkeith, perhaps at the foot of the burgage plots. The river would provide at least a psychological, if not a highly defensible physical barrier. Entrance to and exit from the town would have been either through small gates at the back of the burgage plots or through the main gates, or ports, of the town. There was a West Port by at least the sixteenth century which probably stood on the High Street, in this Area 2; but its exact location is not known.

The impression, from cartographic sources, is that this section of the High Street was less developed than the eastern section, which housed the town's market. Indeed, this area incorporates the glebe lands D, six acres of open land used to support the minister. It stretched along both sides of the Old Edinburgh Road, and is remembered to this day by the name of Glebe Street. According to Lesslie's plan of *c* 1770 **figure 11**, a poor house **H** stood on the east side of the Old Edinburgh Road, north of the glebe, near to the Lugton Bridge. This was erected in 1747 by the Kirk Session.

history

archaeology

was also attracted along the Old Edinburgh Road. The town's West Port, too, may have been in this area, in all probability on the High Street. Due to the lack of any previous archaeological work in Dalkeith, and in the absence of any chance finds from the historic core, only general comments can be made at present about the archaeological potential of Dalkeith.

In comparison with the east or north-east end of the High Street, the western or south-west end shows intense competition for space, particularly the triangular block defined by South Street, Buccleuch Street and High Street. Here, the medieval burgage plots (if they extended this far west) appear to have been broken up for redevelopment, at least by the late eighteenth century. Lesslie's map of *c* 1770 **figure 11** shows this as a congested area, comprising small islands of buildings separated by narrow wynds. South Street itself appears to have originated from a vennel which was widened, probably around the turn of the nineteenth century.

Buildings situated in this part of the old burgh were almost certainly constructed on the site of, or directly over the remains of, earlier buildings, a sequence possibly going back to the medieval period and continuing up to the present day. Although there has been no opportunity to examine, archaeologically, any of the street frontages in Dalkeith, evidence of earlier, possibly medieval structures may be expected to survive, sealed beneath eighteenth- or nineteenth-century standing buildings along the High Street and the vennels leading off it.

In other Scottish towns, archaeological excavations have revealed that street frontages have potential for the preservation of archaeological deposits, in spite of the fact that cellarage may have destroyed some earlier evidence. Recent excavations in Perth, Dunfermline and Arbroath have also shown that the width and alignment of the main streets in the burghs have changed over the centuries. Earlier cobbled street surfaces and contemporary buildings may therefore be preserved up to three or four metres behind the line of the modern street frontage. At the Abbot's House, in Dunfermline, recent excavations uncovered a whole section of the medieval street itself, inside and sealed below the floor of the standing building.

The potential for medieval archaeological levels, particularly earlier buildings, to be preserved beneath present-day standing buildings in this area of Dalkeith is likely to be concentrated along High Street, and between Buccleuch Street and South Street. The limits of the medieval town are uncertain; even as late as the last decades of the eighteenth century the western limit of the burgh was Buccleuch Street. Much of this area is now under the 'Town Centre' development **A** where little archaeological evidence is likely to have survived. Its ground plan, however, has largely reinstated the eighteenth-century street pattern and has preserved the line of vennels; pockets of archaeological deposits may, therefore, survive.

standing buildings

Nos 1–5 London Road are an interesting terrace of *c* 1775 houses, with steps directly from the pavement to the front doors. *Nos* 1 and 2 have forestairs to the rear and *no* 3 is more elaborate with a pediment to the street. Originally built as a terrace of three three-bayed houses, *nos* 1–3 were the homes of Dalkeith merchants. Apparently the work of the same group of masons is *no* 6 London Road. Originally constructed in the later eighteenth century as a three bay house, a fourth bay was later added to its right. Steps, with a wrought iron balustrade, lead up to the central doorway of a panelled door with a two-pane fanlight.

An interesting architectural feature in this area is the Watch Tower **F** in the burial ground on Old Edinburgh Road. Built in the early decades of the nineteenth century by the Committee of Dalkeith Churchyard Association, its purpose was to house overnight armed watchmen, who guarded the graveyard from body snatchers. Nearby stands the

history

West Church **E**. Built in 1840 to a design of William Burn, it is indicative of the growing

archaeology

The High Street itself was the centre of activity in the medieval burgh, and its archaeological potential should not be forgotten when considering, for example, environmental improvements or the insertion or renewal of services. Evidence of medieval street levels may be preserved, either as metalled surfaces or as accumulated midden deposits. The remains of other important features of the medieval townscape may also be sealed beneath the present road surface, for example the remains of the West Port might well survive in this area. Any ground disturbance of the smaller wynds should also be monitored archaeologically as a matter of routine.

Behind the High Street frontage were the backlands of the burgage plots. Over time, these were gradually built over as pressure for space within the town increased. Evidence of burgage plots can survive, buried beneath modern buildings and car parks; and they are an extremely valuable source of information as they often provide evidence of the activities and conditions of everyday life in a medieval town. Excavations in other medieval towns in Scotland, such as Perth, Aberdeen and St Andrews, have revealed middens, rubbish pits, cess pits and vegetable plots as common features of medieval backlands, alongside craft workshops and kilns.

The ends of the burgage plots were sometimes marked by small walls, wooden fences or ditches, beyond which may have been a back lane. On the north side of the High Street in Area 2, the plots appear to have extended down to the glebe, of which Glebe Street is a reminder. The proliferation of vennels and the effects of repletion on the north side of the High Street make it difficult to determine the nature of the plots here. Any further developments here should be archaeologically monitored as remnants of the burgage plots themselves, their boundaries and the activities which took place within them may be preserved below ground.

Several changes have been made to the town plan over the last 200 years or so, to aid access into the town and to provide extra housing, but these modern developments may conceal medieval features. The Edinburgh Road was built in the late eighteenth or early nineteenth century and provides the most direct route into town from the Lugton Bridge. Lesslie's *c* 1770 map **figure 11** indicates that some earlier buildings may have been demolished to make way for the bridge; their foundations may be preserved below ground.

Lesslie's and Wood's maps **figure 11** *&* **14** both show a number of mills in Dalkeith, two of which are located in Area 2: a waulk mill **J** and a barley mill **I**, although only part of the former has survived. Little is known about medieval mills as few have been excavated (*see also* pp 56–7).

Waulking involves beating wet cloth or tweed in order to make its texture more closely knit and durable prior to dyeing; this process also involved beating fuller's earth into the cloth. Before the advent of the watermill, the cloth was probably trampled in pits. Waulk mills (the Scottish term for fulling mills) have received little archaeological attention, population of the town in the nineteenth century. The swelling congregation in St Nicholas parish church had put pressure on the inadequate accommodation, and so the fifth Duke of Buccleuch gifted the site and built and endowed the church.

mills

Mills had been an important part of Dalkeith's economy since the middle ages. The town had more than one mill by 1540, and at least one of these mills was supplied by water controlled by the 'water yett' that stood on the Hauch of Dalkeith, by a little oak tree, on the way to Braehead. On 1 December 1583, it is recorded that the rentals of the corn mills of Dalkeith were £200, a not insignificant sum, and by 1587, there were four grain and cloth mills in Dalkeith. Lesslie's map indicates a barley mill **I** in Area 2; and, immediately to its west, a waulk mill **J**, a reminder of the growing textile industry in Dalkeith in the eighteenth century.

the cattle market

Dalkeith's role as a grain market was reinforced by its weekly cattle market, held every Tuesday. This brought not merely stock farmers to the town with money to spend, but also provided the town's butchers with the necessary animals to supply the Edinburgh market. On some occasions, it was said, the consumers in the capital took all the meat the Dalkeith butchers could kill. The local craftsmen also took some advantage of the by-products of the butchers' activities (*see above*, p 34). As well as this weekly market, the town also held an annual fair on the third Tuesday of October, catering largely for the trade in horses and black cattle. This may have been held at the foot of South Street, where the cattle market was sited by the early nineteenth century **M**.

history

archaeology

despite the importance of cloth making to medieval and post-medieval economies. In England, no medieval fulling mills have been excavated (although a fuller's house was discovered at Winchester). Only one post-medieval example has been investigated, at Ardingley in Sussex. This sixteenth- or seventeenth-century site is a useful reminder of the possible longevity of mill sites: it began life as a forge before being converted to a fulling mill in the eighteenth century. A full ground plan of the mill was recovered, including the dam, the water channel that drove the wheel, and culverts. All overlay and reused elements of the earlier forge, including the forge anvil and one of the wheel pits, the latter reused to house the water-wheel that drove the fulling mill.

Where there are mills there are also weirs, leats (or lades) and mill races (*see also* **area 1**, p 57). An extensive network of leats and tail races can be seen on Lesslie's *c* 1770 map, all of which have since disappeared. Although the barley mill has also disappeared, the waulk mill appears to have survived, in part, among a group of buildings on the north side of Ironmills Road. Any development here may determine whether their origins pre-date the eighteenth century. The leats and tail races have been backfilled but are likely to be preserved below the present ground surface; the leat appears to be under Ironmills Road. Future developments and environmental improvements along this bank of the North Esk should be routinely monitored.

The essentially rural atmosphere of Dalkeith is also reflected in the number of small fields lying close to the edge of the historic town. As the town expanded in the nineteenth and twentieth centuries, many of these were subsumed by housing developments. Lesslie's map of *c* 1770 **figure 11** shows a patchwork of fields to the west of the Old Edinburgh Road, under what is now Glebe Street and Mitchell Street. Here stood the glebe fields **D**, on either side of the Old Edinburgh Road, and two fields which were probably leased by the mills. The field boundaries have since disappeared but their footings, probably for drystone walls, may survive below present ground level.

area 3

South Street/Brewlands/River South Esk/Musselburgh Road/High Street **figure 21**

description

The south side of the High Street, like the north, is a mixture of the old and the new, with the more recent developments designed specifically to blend in with the old. The tolbooth **figure 12.A** is the oldest civic building in the town. Space set aside for parking along much of this side of the High Street exaggerates what is already a very wide main thoroughfare. Most of the eastern end of the street frontages is taken up with housing, interspersed with a few public houses. Shops predominate along the western end. The main traffic crosses the west end of the High Street, leaving the eastern end quiet and, because of its considerable width, rather empty looking. The entrance to Dalkeith House is imposing; it is a reminder both of the town's links with Dalkeith Palace and its separate existence.

St Andrew Street, which was once a back lane behind the former burgage plots, was the first of the town's high-quality local housing authority housing schemes, constructed in the 1930s. Beyond St Andrew Street, and extending down towards the River South Esk, are much more recent housing developments built over what had been a patchwork of fields. One of these fields still survives largely intact, Brewlands **B**, which lies to the south of Newmills Road.

The western end of this area is marked by South Street, once a narrow wynd widened to allow increased traffic. The early nineteenth-century frontages here contrast with the modern 'Town Centre' on the opposite side of South Street (*see* p 59). One of the few wynds or vennels remaining in the medieval core of the town **D** runs behind the South Street frontage, creating a triangular block of properties, and links High Street and St Andrew Street.

historical background

High Street and the townscape

Dalkeith town was, for much of its history, essentially one street, called the High Street, running approximately east to west, away from the castle. By 1430, and probably of very much earlier date, this main street, originally called 'the great road', was established and lined with burgage plots. A number of vennels or wynds ran from the High Street. Lining the street were the tenements and burgage plots of the burgesses. It is interesting that these plots were commonly called 'cottage lands', 'cotlands', 'cottage tenements',

archaeological potential and future development

The most recent Dalkeith Local Plan (1980) is now largely out of date and many of the planning proposals contained within it have already been implemented. It does, however, state that a few edge-of-town sites are suitable for office or housing developments and that gap sites within the town would be utilised. Due to the lack of any previous archaeological work in Dalkeith, and in the absence of any chance finds from the historic core, only general comments can be made at present about the archaeological potential of the town.

Area 3 includes the High Street, the core of the medieval town. Buildings situated in the core of the old burgh were almost certainly constructed on the site of, or directly over the remains of, earlier buildings, a sequence possibly going back to the medieval period and continuing up to the present day. Although there has been no opportunity to examine, archaeologically, any of the street frontages in Dalkeith, evidence of earlier, possibly medieval structures may be expected to survive, sealed beneath eighteenth- or nineteenth-century standing buildings along the High Street and the vennels leading off it, such as South Street.

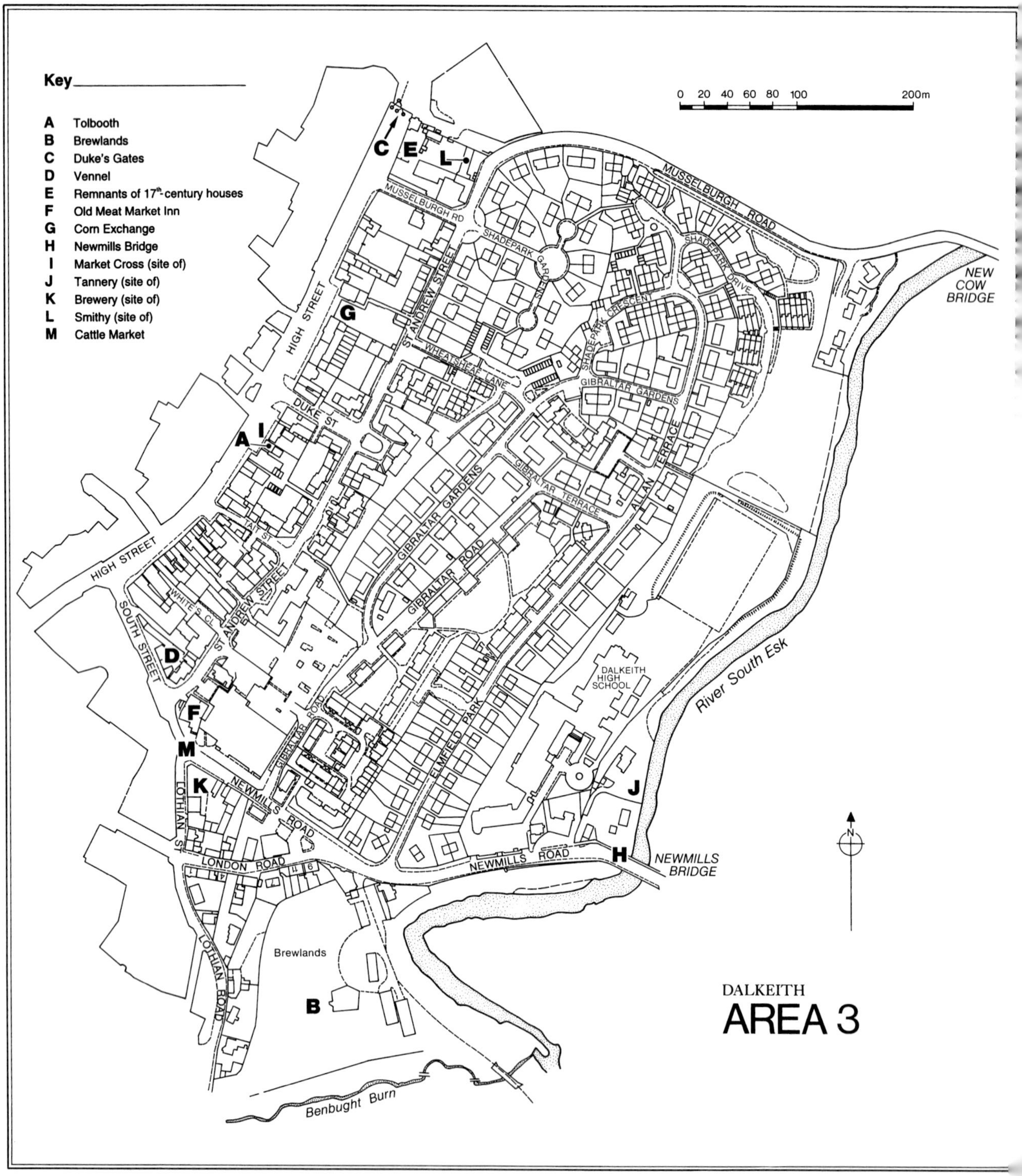
Key
A Tolbooth
B Brewlands
C Duke's Gates
D Vennel
E Remnants of 17th-century houses
F Old Meat Market Inn
G Corn Exchange
H Newmills Bridge
I Market Cross (site of)
J Tannery (site of)
K Brewery (site of)
L Smithy (site of)
M Cattle Market
0 20 40 60 80 100 200m
MUSSELBURGH ROAD
MUSSELBURGH RD
SHADEPARK DRIVE
SHADEPARK CRESCENT
GIBRALTAR GARDENS
ALLAN TERRACE
GIBRALTAR TERRACE
GIBRALTAR ROAD
WHEATSHEAF LANE
ST ANDREW STREET
HIGH STREET
DUKE ST
TAIT ST
WHITE'S CL
SOUTH STREET
NEWMILLS ROAD
LONDON ROAD
LOTHIAN ST
LOTHIAN ROAD
EDMFIELD PARK
DALKEITH HIGH SCHOOL
River South Esk
NEW COW BRIDGE
NEWMILLS BRIDGE
Brewlands
Benbught Burn
N
DALKEITH
AREA 3

figure 21
Area 3

'husbandlands' or 'husband tenements', rather than tofts, rigs or burgage plots, as is the norm in burghs of this period. This is probably a reflection of the predominantly agricultural nature of the town.

There is no evidence that the town was encircled with walls, although many medieval Scottish towns surrounded themselves with ditches and palisading. It is quite probable that this was also the case in Dalkeith. This would provide at least a psychological, if not a highly defensible physical barrier. Entrance to and exit from the town would have been either through small gates at the back of the burgage plots or through the main gates, or ports, of the town. It is known that there was a West Port by at least the sixteenth century (*see* p 60 **area 2**); but no reference has yet been found to an East Port, which may have stood in this Area 3 or, more probably, within the grounds of Dalkeith Palace.

The gateway to the estate from the High Street, the Duke's Gates **C**, was erected in 1784 by James Playfair. The four square piers are linked by a screen wall, with the gateway of cast iron, with leaf design, at the centre. They form an imposing definition of the separateness of estate and town, notwithstanding the close links forged over the centuries (*passim*). Close by, a scarcely discernible clue to the seventeenth-century past may be seen in the south wall that flanks the entrance from the High Street to the Dalkeith Estate. Blocked windows and doorways **E** are the sole reminder of the physical closeness of the homes of townspeople and of their ducal neighbours. They also imply that the wall incorporates the front (or back) walls of now demolished houses, the remains of which may lie hidden below present ground level.

Closes ran back from the High Street, on both sides, and gradually became developed with dwellings and workshops. Visitors to Dalkeith commented favourably on the townscape. Daniel Defoe wrote in 1724 that the 'town [was] spacious, and well built, and [was] the better, no doubt, for the neighbourhood of so many noblemen's and gentlemen's

history

archaeology

Nineteenth-century buildings may also incorporate earlier structures. These may be represented by floor surfaces and other features associated with earlier phases of occupation, sealed beneath the modern floor levels, or survive as structural elements, for instance, walls that have reused earlier foundations. Similarly, buildings which have more than one phase of construction may have earlier structural features sealed within the fabric itself, hidden by later additions. The present tolbooth **A**, for example, the oldest building on this side of the High Street and a Scheduled Ancient Monument, dates to the later seventeenth century, but may have been built on the site of an earlier tolbooth. It was probably refaced in the nineteenth century; and was refurbished and converted to a church hall in the 1960s, although features such as the weigh room and pit prison survive. The archaeological potential both of the tolbooth itself and its immediate vicinity is very high. Any ground disturbance within or close to the tolbooth, and any future works within the building itself, will require archaeological supervision.

In other Scottish towns, archaeological excavations have revealed that street frontages offer the highest potential for the preservation of archaeological deposits, in spite of the fact that evidence may have been destroyed by the construction of cellars. Recent excavations in Perth, Dunfermline and Arbroath have also shown that the width and alignment of the main streets in the burghs have changed over the centuries. Earlier cobbled street surfaces and contemporary buildings may, therefore, be preserved up to three or four metres behind the line of the modern street frontage. At Abbot House, in Dunfermline, recent excavations uncovered a whole section of the medieval street itself, inside and sealed below the floor of the standing building; up to six phases of street surfaces were revealed, each separated by thick dumps of midden. Here, archaeology has clearly demonstrated how dramatically street frontages can shift over time, and highlighted the potential for archaeological deposits to be buried below later buildings. The potential for medieval archaeological levels, particularly earlier buildings, to be preserved beneath present-day standing buildings in Dalkeith is likely to be concentrated along High Street, but South Street and the smaller vennels should also be considered.

houses of such eminence in the neighbourhood'. By the end of the eighteenth century it was said of the town that it was 'though not a royal borough ... a considerable place ... it contain[ed] one very handsome street, beside lanes'. Eighteenth-century maps also suggest that the increase in population had little effect on the street pattern. In any town, the street lay-out is the most enduring topographical feature. The main street was by now fully built up, and there is cartographic evidence of repletion, or building in the backlands. This was more marked on the south side of the street than on the north.

At the rear of the High Street properties, there was a back lane which, by the early nineteenth century, was formalised into a thoroughfare called Back Lane or Back Street, now St Andrew Street. Still respecting the early street pattern is the Old Meal Market Inn **F** at *nos* 2–4 St Andrew Street **figure 13**. This was built by the owner of a brewery that once stood opposite. The lean-to porch is a replacement for an original external forestair. The adjoining arcaded former cartshed functioned in the nineteenth century as a smithy, although little of its original character now remains. The main dwelling was converted into an inn in 1874.

the market place, markets and fairs

The High Street is wide at this north-eastern section. This is because it functioned as the important market place for Dalkeith; and it was here that the market cross stood **I**. In 1401, Robert III (1390–1406) granted to Sir James Douglas of Dalkeith that his 'villa' should be held as a free burgh of barony. (In 1540, it was elevated to the status of a burgh of regality.) Presumably having the right to hold a market, one of the basic rights of

history

archaeology

A double circle of stones, near the centre of the High Street, marks the site of the old market cross of Dalkeith **I**. This is a useful reminder that the High Street itself was the centre of activity and its archaeological potential should not be forgotten when considering, for example, environmental improvements, or the insertion or renewal of services. Not only may evidence of the medieval streets be preserved beneath the present road surface, but so may the remains of other important features of the medieval townscape—the market cross itself, ports and wells—of which no archaeological evidence has yet been found. The smaller wynds should also be monitored routinely.

Behind the High Street frontage were the backlands of the burgage plots. Over time, these were gradually built over as pressure for space within the town increased. Evidence of burgage plots, however, can survive, buried beneath modern buildings and car parks. Burgage plots are an extremely valuable source of information because they often document the activities and conditions of everyday life in a medieval town. Excavations in other medieval burghs, such as Perth, Aberdeen and St Andrews, have revealed that middens, rubbish pits, cess pits and vegetable plots are common features of medieval backlands, alongside craft workshops and kilns. A series of three excavations at Canal Street in Perth, for example, showed that the boundaries of these plots were shifted regularly, revealing a fascinating sequence of continually changing plot boundaries, reflecting the amalgamation and sub-division of properties throughout the medieval period.

The end of the burgage plots was often marked by small walls, wooden fences or ditches, and beyond that, a back lane. At the rear of the tenements on the south side of High Street, the back lane ran approximately where St Andrew Street is today. Any proposed development or other significant ground disturbance in the former backlands of the High Street and St Andrew Street should be archaeologically monitored, as remnants of the burgage plots themselves, their boundaries and the activities which took place within them, may be preserved below ground.

Lesslie's and Wood's maps **figures 11 & 14** both show a number of industrial sites in Dalkeith, some of which lie in Area 3. These industries were also common in the medieval period and may have been long established here. A tannery **J** is shown close to the bank burghs, the town would have attracted traders from the surrounding rural hinterland. Increased trade meant increased prosperity, not only for the burgh superior, but for the town itself. Some of the grain sold at the weekly corn market, held on a Sunday until 1581, when it was transferred to a Tuesday, was grown by the burgesses on land around the burgh. By this time Dalkeith was functioning as a market centre for many rural settlements in the vicinity.

Other markets were, clearly, still held on a Sunday, as in 1583 the Edinburgh magistrates enacted that none of their burgesses should attend any Sunday markets in neighbouring towns, including Dalkeith. The markets would not be merely for the buying and selling of victuals. The local craftsmen, such as the cutler, John Lytoun, an indweller in the town in 1576, the wrights who were also employed on the crown's business, the coopers and the smiths would sell their products. The town obviously had numerous baxters, brewers, fleshers and cadgers, necessary not only to supply the palace, but also the national army and troops so often billeted in the town in the sixteenth to eighteenth centuries (*see* pp 21–39). The town also had the right to hold a fair. This would attract merchants from much further afield in Scotland, and from abroad. From 1581, its appointed date was 10 October.

Fairs and weekly markets continued throughout the seventeenth century in spite of the upheaval of billeted troops and the like. Occasional crises, such as plague in Preston and Prestonpans meant that the markets and fairs of Dalkeith, along with those of Haddington, Preston and Tranent, were banned for some six weeks or so in 1636. Such setbacks did not prevent the emergence of Dalkeith as an important market. Nor is it surprising that there should have been so many grain mills and ancillary buildings in the

history

archaeology

of the River South Esk, in what are now the grounds of the school. Here, a series of wooden tanks, set into the ground, would have contained batches of hides soaking in various solutions. Lime was used to strip the hides of flesh and hair; and then animal dung (dog dung in particular) and vegetable extracts were used to de-lime the skins. Finally, they were soaked in a solution of water and bark for up to eighteen months to preserve the leather and inhibit fungal decay. The tannery at Dalkeith is probably of eighteenth-century origin, but there may have been a tannery on or near this same spot for centuries. A recent excavation on the site of the present visitors' centre at St Andrews Castle in Fife revealed the remains of a fourteenth-century tannery, comprising a series of wood-lined pits housed within an open barn. This discovery has demonstrated that the techniques employed in tanning remained more or less unchanged until the advent of chemicals in relatively modern times. Another tannery, this time of late eighteenth-century date, was recently excavated in Crieff.

Other industrial sites in Area 3 include a smithy **L** at the north-east end of the High Street. A medieval smithy was also found in Perth in 1983, in a specifically industrial zone on the very edge of the medieval town (Meal Vennel). Large amounts of slag and waste material were found, as well as the stone base of the anvil itself. Brewing and malting were common occupations in medieval towns and Dalkeith was no exception; a brewery **K** was located on the corner of Lothian Road and South Street. Excavations at Canal Street, Perth, in 1985, also uncovered a malting kiln and a coble (a clay-lined pit) in the backlands of a burgage plot, dating to the late fourteenth or early fifteenth century. Barley was steeped in a coble until germination, and then dried by hot air in a malting kiln. The malted barley was then ready to be used in brewing.

What appears to have been a kiln was discovered in Dalkeith in the early nineteenth century, although its exact location is unknown (the only grid reference is NT 33 67). Within a small stone-built circular structure, discovered by workmen digging the foundations for a new house, were bones, ashes and a stone mould for casting buckles **figure 22** (published in the *Proceedings of the Society of Antiquaries of Scotland*, 1851–54). Eight different buckles were represented altogether, all of seventeenth-century type; the mould was donated to the National Museums of Scotland by the then owner of the property, Mr

figure 22
Two sides of a seventeenth-century buckle mould

history

town (*see* pp 56 & 62). Apart from the obvious natural geographical advantage of a superb water supply, it was said of Dalkeith, in 1724, that it was a 'pretty large market-town, and the better market for being so near to Edinburgh; for there comes great quantities of provisions here from the southern countries, which are brought up here to be carried to Edinburgh market again, and sold there'. One of the most important commodities brought to Dalkeith was grain. Indeed, it was said that Dalkeith was 'perhaps the greatest grain market in Scotland'; and that this grain, once sold, brought 'ready' money, which the farmers then spent in the town. Some of the grain was transported to the west, to supply such towns as Carron, Glasgow and Paisley. Clearly this weekly market, held on a Thursday, functioned as an important distribution point. As well as this Thursday market, there was also a meal market, held every Monday from Martinmas to Whitsun.

Dalkeith's role as a grain market was reinforced by its weekly cattle market, held every Tuesday. This brought not merely stock farmers to the town with money to spend, but also provided the town's butchers with the necessary animals to supply the Edinburgh market. On some occasions, it was said, the consumers in the capital took all the meat the Dalkeith butchers could kill. The local craftsmen also took some advantage of the by-products of the butchers' activities (*see above*, p 34). As well as this weekly market, the town

archaeology

John Gray. Despite the presence of this buckle mould in the kiln, it may be that the kiln fulfilled another purpose. The quantities of calcined bone found with the stone mould suggest that, at least in its last phase, the kiln was being used to make fertiliser; calcined bone was, and still is, used as fertiliser.

The essentially rural atmosphere of Dalkeith is reflected in the number of small fields lying close to the edge of the historic town. As the town expanded in the nineteenth and twentieth centuries, many of these were subsumed by housing developments. Their held an annual fair on the third Tuesday of October, catering largely for the trade in horses and black cattle. This may have been held at the foot of South Street, where the cattle market was sited by the early nineteenth century **M**.

standing buildings

The market place, market cross, tolbooth and tron (weigh-beam) were the secular focal points of the town (*see* p 25). A tolbooth had been in existence from at least the sixteenth century. Dalkeith's tolbooth **figure 12** *&* **A** (176–180 High Street, now protected as a Scheduled Ancient Monument), fronting the widened High Street, the site of the market place (*see* p 32), is a visual reminder of the crucial role that the market held in Dalkeith's past. It was in the tolbooth that market dues were collected and the public weighbeam was housed. The present building was erected in the second half of the seventeenth century, probably being reworked to some extent in the eighteenth century, and retains many of its original exterior features, although the frontage was probably refaced in the nineteenth century. The whole building underwent refurbishment in 1966. The panel above the doorway, with the date 1648 and the arms of the earl of Buccleuch, is misleading. It was discovered in the grounds of Dalkeith Palace in the late eighteenth century, and only at that time placed on the tolbooth façade. The tolbooth also functioned as the town's court house, the court room on the first floor having a coffered ceiling. It was here, also, that the town's prison was housed. This consisted of a pit hole in the subterranean basement, and an upper prison. Dalkeith's gibbet stood in front of the tolbooth, where the second last public hanging in Scotland took place in 1827.

The Corn Exchange **figure 16** *&* **G**, built in the mid nineteenth century, although now somewhat dilapidated, epitomises Dalkeith's function as an important market town. Built by public subscription, it was the largest indoor grain market in Scotland.

Newmills Bridge **H**, at the south of Area 3, was built in 1756 to afford a crossing over the South Esk. It was widened and repaired in 1812, and largely reconstructed in the late 1830s, when three new arches were thrown over it to facilitate movement south. Nearby stands the earlier mill, Newmills. Built in 1703, by the mid nineteenth century it formed part of a larger complex, with a mill lade that was blocked by 1892. The South Esk, as well as the North Esk, was a first rate source of power; and the tannery and mills are testament to the ability of the Dalkeith people to harness this source.

history

archaeology

boundaries, however, probably in the form of drystone walls, may be preserved. Lesslie's map of *c* 1770 **figure 11** shows a patchwork of fields between St Andrew Street and the River South Esk, under what is now Gibraltar Gardens, Gibraltar Road, Elmfield Park and Allan Terrace housing developments. One particular field, which lies south of London Road/Newmills Road, is still known as 'Brewlands' **B**, and undoubtedly provided barley for the maltmen and brewers who are known to have been operating in the town by the sixteenth century.

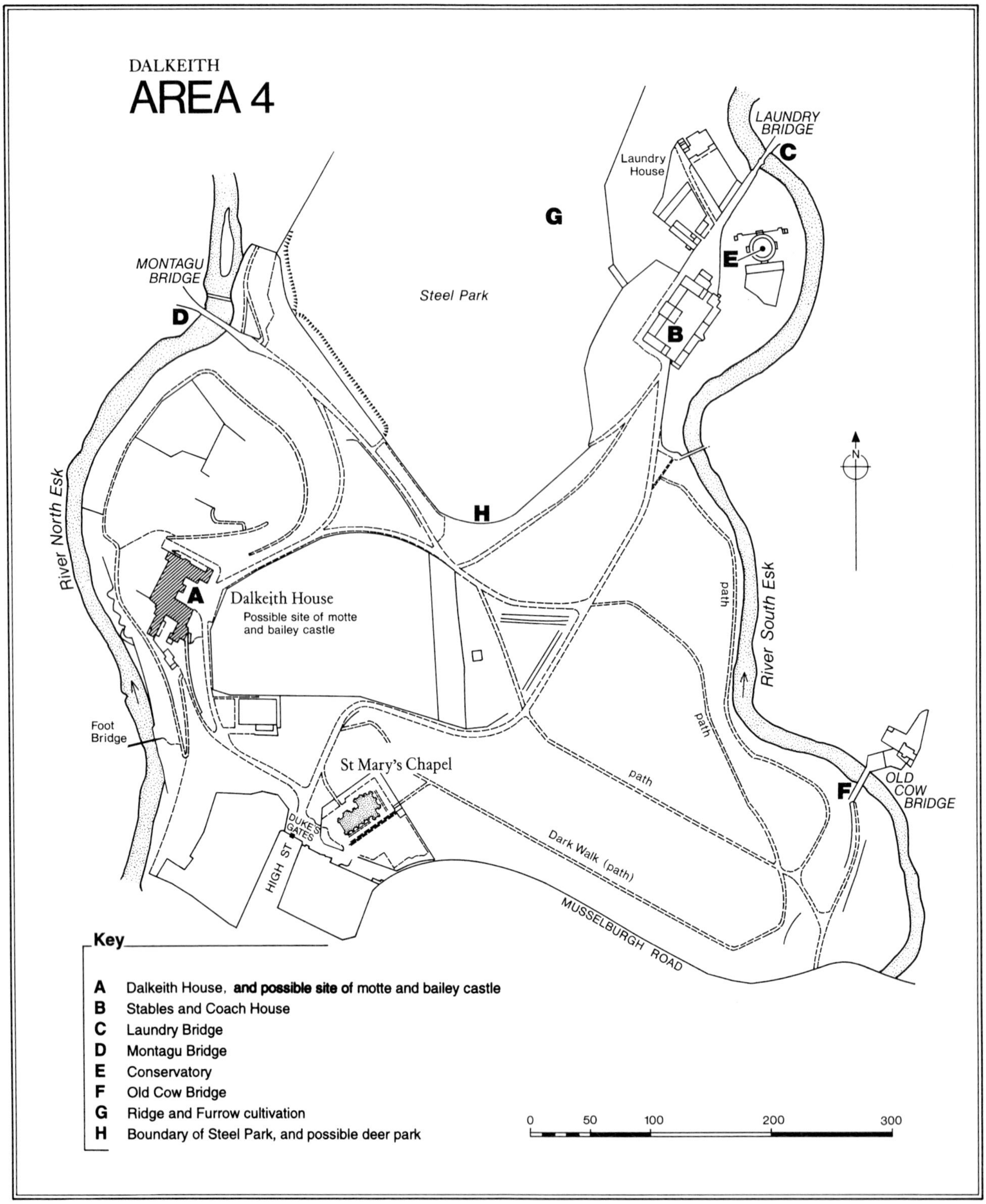
DALKEITH
AREA 4
LAUNDRY BRIDGE
C
Laundry House
G
E
MONTAGU BRIDGE
Steel Park
D
B
H
River North Esk
A
Dalkeith House
Possible site of motte and bailey castle
River South Esk
path
path
path
Foot Bridge
St Mary's Chapel
F
OLD COW BRIDGE
DUKE'S GATES
HIGH ST
Dark Walk (path)
MUSSELBURGH ROAD
N
Key
A Dalkeith House, and possible site of motte and bailey castle
B Stables and Coach House
C Laundry Bridge
D Montagu Bridge
E Conservatory
F Old Cow Bridge
G Ridge and Furrow cultivation
H Boundary of Steel Park, and possible deer park
0 50 100 200 300

GD03032G/1998

figure 23
Area 4

area 4

Musselburgh Road/River South Esk/Laundry Bridge/Steel Park/River North Esk/Dalkeith House grounds **figure 23**

description

This area comprises Dalkeith House **A** and its grounds (currently leased to the University of Wisconsin), and the southern end of Dalkeith Parks. Dotted around the grounds are a number of sites and architectural features which provide a useful reminder that this was one of Scotland's premier classical houses and included no less than four bridges across the Esk, a conservatory, chapel, stables, an ice-house, a grassed amphitheatre, wrought iron gateways and paths.

historical background

Dalkeith Castle and Palace

The first mention of Dalkeith occurs *c* 1143. Some time around this date, David I (1124–53) granted various lands to Holyrood Abbey, including the 'land of Dolchet [Dalkeith] between the woods and the open land in the estate of Ruchale [which had been given to the monks of nearby Newbattle]'. The lands of Dalkeith were referred to, again, in a charter of Alwin, abbot of Holyrood, who was abbot prior to 1150. The abbey of Holyrood had received its charter of foundation in 1128, from the same king. One of the witnesses to this charter was William de Graham, and it is known that in the twelfth century the Graham family held Dalkeith. If they had a fortified residence here by this time, it probably suggests that there was settlement at Dalkeith. Not only would a castle offer a measure of protection to those who clustered near its gate, but also the occupants of the castle would require the services of more menial persons and a local food supply would be a necessity. Both of these factors would have attracted settlement close by. This probably means that this early settlement was sited somewhere in the present Dalkeith Parks.

There is no information on the form of this early castle but it may well have been of motte and bailey type (*see below*). Although protected to the north by the rocky fall to the River North Esk, it would have had little natural protection to the south. If a motte existed, then it might later have been converted to a stone castle, the simplest of which merely replaced existing timber defences. This would have comprised a stone curtain wall within which a range of buildings, probably of timber, would have stood around an open central courtyard (*see* **figure 6**).

archaeological potential

The archaeological potential of this area mainly concerns the various phases of Dalkeith House itself, but also includes some specific features within the grounds. It should be borne in mind that early urban settlement might well have been located within the grounds of the present Dalkeith estate, which appears to have gradually encroached on lands used by the townspeople.

Dalkeith House **A**, as it stands today, is the product of several phases of construction covering some seven centuries. Structural elements of any or indeed all the earlier phases might be contained within the fabric of the standing building or lie beneath floor level. Any episodes of ground disturbance within Dalkeith House or its immediate environs, or major refurbishments to the present structure, would merit archaeological monitoring.

At its core is an early castle, dating probably to the twelfth century. Documentary references to great depths of top soil might suggest the spread remnants of a medieval motte. A motte is an earthen, flat-topped mound on which a wooden tower would have

It is to be expected that the castle had a chapel. It has been argued, elsewhere (*see* p 20), that the castle did have a chapel; that chaplainries dedicated to the Virgin Mary and John the Baptist had been established in it by 1377 (although there may be here an element of confusion with St Nicholas Chapel); and that a further chaplainry was endowed in the castle in 1384.

The owners of Dalkeith Castle **figure 6**, the Douglas family, from 1457 also the earls of Morton, were of sufficient importance on the political scene that the township was to participate in many national events, some welcome and others disastrous for the peace of the settlement. Dalkeith was, for example, attacked in the disorder that ensued after the murder of the eighth earl of Douglas in 1452; and there is evidence that the town was to be sacked and burned on many more occasions in the sixteenth century (*see* p 23). The castle was, however, of sufficient grandeur by this time that it was often host to royalty. The presence of nobility and the royal retinue would not only have been a common sight in the town, but would also provide employment and a market for supplies.

It is known, for example, that James II (1437–60) had been resident in Dalkeith in 1444. The second earl of Morton, John Douglas, was one of the nobles who met Princess Margaret, eldest daughter of Henry VII of England (1485–1509), in 1503 at Lamberton Kirk in the Borders and escorted her to Newbattle Abbey, less than 2 km south of Dalkeith, on her route to meet her husband, King James IV (1488–1513). It was at Dalkeith Castle that King James met his future bride. The couple remained there for four days, the king returning daily from Edinburgh and affairs of state. A serious fire took hold at this time, probably in the stables of the castle as the new queen's horses were killed and all their bridles and gear destroyed.

Dalkeith Castle was considered a worthy place of residence for King James V (1513–42) and his court, in September 1519, when fear of plague forced them out of Edinburgh. The castle was often the resting place for royalty during this century; and the townspeople must have found the royal retinue and noblemen a common site. In 1525, in the following year at Christmas, and in 1536, James V's court was in residence there. Mary, Queen of Scots (1542–67), spent a few days there in October/November 1565. The privy council was held in the town on numerous occasions during the reign of James VI (1567–1625). In April 1601, the king decided that the council, called for the 30th of the month in Linlithgow should meet, instead, in Dalkeith. His main, stated, reason for this was that many of those called to the council lived nearby and residents of Edinburgh could travel home for the night. There must, however, have been many occasions over the previous century when the people of Dalkeith were called upon to provide board and lodgings.

The fourth earl, James Douglas, took a central stage in Scottish politics (for a while as Regent Morton), until his execution in 1581; but not before rebuilding the castle and converting it into a Scottish Renaissance palace, described as 'magnificent' and called,

history

archaeology

stood. A palisade around the top edge of the mound would have provided extra defence. An outer, defensive ditch would have surrounded the base of the mound, the upcast from which formed the fabric of the motte itself. Mottes often have an outer enclosure, or bailey, which contained most of the domestic buildings and structures; it was only during an attack that the tower on the motte itself was occupied. There is also a nineteenth-century tradition that the lawns which now stand in front of Dalkeith Palace were formed only after the infilling of a river course that ran in front of the palace; this might be evidence of a moat. If a motte existed at Dalkeith, it may later have been converted to a stone castle, the simplest of which merely replaced existing timber defences. This would have comprised a stone curtain wall, within which a range of buildings, probably of timber, would have stood around an open central courtyard.

This would later have been extended or incorporated into a larger structure, comprising a tower house, probably with a barmkin or enclosure. In the 1570s, a major phase of rebuilding converted the then existing castle into a palace. Slezer's view of the castle in 1698 **figure 8** shows the tower house and two ranges of buildings. The inner contemporaneously, the 'Lion's Den', where he entertained the king 'with great honour' in 1579 **figure 8**. The precise design of this palace is uncertain, although remnants of it form part of the present Dalkeith House (*see* pp 74–5). It is known that as well as being a sumptuous residence, it also had a castle yard, as it was here, under the ground, that Morton allegedly hid his treasure. The depiction of Dalkeith Palace by Slezer over a hundred years later probably reveals a strong likeness to the palace as it was in Morton's time, showing as it does the remnants of an earlier tower structure in the corner **figure 8**.

Within nine days of Morton's death, King James VI entered the palace, from the parish church of St Nicholas, with two pipers leading his procession. Morton's lands, including Dalkeith, were forfeit to the crown and bestowed on Esmé Stewart, later Duke of Lennox. He resided in Dalkeith Castle for a while, before his departure and death in France in 1583. The following year, the attainder was reversed and the lands of Dalkeith reverted back to the house of Douglas.

In 1589, it was claimed that the king would borrow Dalkeith for his new queen, Anna of Denmark, to stay in, as it was 'the nighest fair house to Edinburgh'. It was again mooted that it would be one of the places James VI would take his queen in March 1591; the local people were instructed to supply 'meit, drink and ludgeing at their reasonable expenses'. He was certainly in residence there in March 1592, when Edinburgh was instructed to furnish him with twenty soldiers for a month to wait on him at Dalkeith; and again on 9 August, 1592; and it was in the palace that his wife gave birth to a daughter on Christmas Eve, 1598. On this occasion, the revelry at the court offended some Protestant ministers of the kirk. It was said, by a visitor to Dalkeith a century later, that Queen Anna kept her court there during the absences of the king. This may be correct; but a contemporary account, in 1592, noted that the queen was to retire to Dalkeith, 'where she likes not to abide'.

Visits to the castle were not always peaceable. For a while in 1542 Cardinal David Beaton was warded in Dalkeith Castle, for his opposition to the proposed marriage of the young Queen Mary with Prince Edward, the son of Henry VIII of England (1509–47). The choice of Dalkeith was determined by the fact that it was 'a very strong house'. The castle was besieged and taken by the governor, James, second earl of Arran, in 1543. Expenses are detailed in the *Treasurer's Accounts* not merely for the siege of the castle, but also for its provisioning thereafter. Four years later, in 1547, the town was once again to witness the devastation of war, when hundreds of fugitives fled to Dalkeith after the disastrous defeat of the Scots at the Battle of Pinkie; and in the same year the garrison at Dalkeith Castle, under Sir George Douglas, fell to an English siege. In 1548 the town was burned by the English; and 'the house of Dalkeith was destroyed'. On 8 June 1550, it was reported that Dalkeith, along with other towns, was subject to 'birning, utir hirschip and distructioun' by the English, which is probably a reference to the 1548 attack. On the

range, with the tower-house set in one corner, was grouped around an inner, enclosed courtyard. The outer range was grouped around a courtyard open at one end. Both courtyards were entered through ornate gate-houses. In the early eighteenth century the palace was converted into a fashionable, and lavish, country house. Although the south-eastern courtyard wall was removed to form a U-plan mansion, much of the earlier palace was absorbed into the new structure. This was the last major phase of rebuilding, although there were internal alterations in the 1830s.

There are references to parks at Dalkeith and to the walling of parks in the seventeenth century, although the nature and date of their establishment is uncertain. In 1637, Charles I expressed a wish to buy the palace and to turn 8,000 acres of land into a deer park, but at what date, if ever, a deer park was established is uncertain. The creation of deer parks, a practice also known as emparking, was common in the middle ages; there is documentary evidence that one existed at nearby Newbattle Abbey in the thirteenth century. On average, areas of between 150 and 300 acres were enclosed within a bank crowned by a timber palisade, often with an internal ditch. At Cold Overton, in

28th, Captain William Stewart was posted, with 500 men, 'for resistance to the English'. The town was also to be used as the base, in 1560, for the Protestant Lords of the Congregation, when in opposition to the Roman Catholic regent, Mary of Guise. During the subsequent civil war, following the deposition of her daughter, Queen Mary, in 1567, Dalkeith suffered considerable disruption, not least because the Earl of Morton was a leading figure in the king's party, supporting the young King James VI. During this period, the town ordnance and artillery were stored in the church; and in February 1572, Dalkeith was twice burned by a group of attackers, destroying many houses and all the corn of Morton, who would become regent in 1572.

Once the Scottish monarchs had moved to London, Dalkeith was to see royalty more rarely. James VI visited it twice in 1617, on his return to Scotland. Charles I spent a night at the palace during his progress to Edinburgh in June 1633. He found Dalkeith Palace and estate sufficiently attractive that, in 1637, he wished to purchase it in order to turn the 8,000 acres into a deer park, but the transaction was never concluded. A year later, in the wake of unrest over liturgy, the privy council moved from Linlithgow, having virtually abandoned the capital the previous year, to Dalkeith; and the 'Honours of Scotland' were housed at Dalkeith for a while, before their return to Edinburgh.

It was to Dalkeith that all the Scottish and English commissioners of shires were called in 1651 to assent to the Cromwellian Union. Dalkeith was to have close links with Lieutenant General Monck, the Cromwellian officer who was later to become Commander-in-Chief in Scotland, as he leased the palace for five years from 1654, paying as rental £110 for the park and a mere three pence annually for the palace. The commissioners, on the other hand, had paid no rental during their stay earlier in the decade; but goods left by them in Dalkeith Palace were put up for sale in 1653. Occupation by officials of the Protectorate may have been one factor in the adequate upkeep of the furbishings of Dalkeith Palace during these disturbed times. It was considered to be of sufficient luxury that it was emptied to furnish Holyroodhouse for Charles II (1660–85) in 1663.

In 1642, the palace had been sold to Francis, earl of Buccleuch, in an attempt by Morton to clear some of his vast debts. There were to be close links between royalty and the Buccleuch family. The Duchess Anne married the son of Charles II, James, duke of Monmouth. A room in Dalkeith Palace was lavishly furnished for this occasion, entirely at the expense of Charles II. Anne, duchess of Buccleuch, returned from England sometime around 1701 and immediately set about upgrading the family home. James Smith was commissioned to design and effect the alterations. This new eighteenth-century palace incorporated a number of the features of Morton's original. The south-eastern courtyard wall was demolished and parts of the earlier building were absorbed, particularly in the south-western corner and probably also in the north and west wings. This U-plan

history

---

archaeology

Leicestershire, for example, a 200-acre deer park, first recorded in 1296, is enclosed by a bank which still survives in places up to thirty feet wide. These hunting reserves were very popular in the thirteenth century and were exclusively a manifestation of wealth and social status. Deer parks were also compartmented, with internal fences separating, for example, livestock and coppiced areas from hunting reserves. The internal features of deer parks are often the first to be lost to archaeology, but it is common for outer boundaries to survive, sometimes preserved in more recent fence and wall lines. This appears to be the case at Dalkeith, where the perimeter of a probable deer park is preserved in the southern boundary of the present-day Steel Park **H**. This curiously curving boundary bears all the hallmarks of a medieval deer park: a rectangular enclosure with rounded corners. A large and impressive internal ditch still survives and the outer bank is now lined with trees. A substantial wall has been built into the inner face of the bank, but may be a later feature. The topography of the land largely determines the boundaries of the park, since there is a steep drop down to both rivers. The northern boundary of the park is probably the line shown on Lesslie's map of *c* 1770 **figure 11**, mansion had one of the earliest classical façades in Scotland. The lavishness of the interior and the trappings that accompanied it were of equal grandeur. Repair and refacing by John Adam took place in 1762–3, and it is possible that some of the detailed richness comes from this time. Later in the century, in the 1780s, a few alterations were effected, including the addition of a bow-fronted library in the east range, by William Playfair. Further modifications were effected in 1831 by William Burn, although most of his original design was not adopted.

Other features in Dalkeith Park still stand as testament to the grandeur and importance of the house of Buccleuch. The stables and coach-house **B**, designed by William Adam, were erected in 1740. The complex could accommodate about sixty horses, carriages and the staff required to work them. Nearby are the eighteenth-century (or possibly early nineteenth-century) classical laundry and laundry bridge **C**. Montagu Bridge **D**, spanning the North Esk, was designed by Robert Adam and constructed by his brother James in 1792. Three huge life-sized sculptures of stags were originally prominent features along the bridge parapet, but these were removed as they frightened the horses. The bridge was erected by the third duke to celebrate the inheritance by his wife of the Montagu estates. The remnants of a magnificent conservatory **E** still stand, near to the stable block. It was built *c* 1832 to a design of William Burn and was used to grow mediterranean-type fruits, such as oranges and figs; its cavernous basement housed a boiler which heated the glass structure.

St Mary's Chapel

St Mary's Chapel (now St Mary's Episcopal Church) stands inside the Duke's Gates. Built about 1835, as the Buccleuch family's private chapel, to a design of William Burn and David Bryce, the church houses a unique hydraulic organ and bell-ringing mechanism. The magnificent interior, with Minton tile floors and superb stained glass windows, is a reminder of the wealth and status of the Buccleuch family in the nineteenth century. The chapel was transferred to the congregation in 1958.

the physical boundary between palace and town

The palace (castle) and park of Dalkeith would have continued to dominate the landscape. It is unclear when a large stone boundary wall between town and castle was erected. In 1619 a contract was made for a wall to be built round the wood of Dalkeith; but there is no mention of the park surrounding the castle in this document. When the lordship, barony and regality of Dalkeith was transferred to Francis, earl of Buccleuch, in

history

1642, it was described as 'extensive lands, lordship, regality, town and burgh of barony

archaeology

extending across the narrowest gap between the two branches of the river (near to Laundry Bridge **C**). This boundary has disappeared, but there are enough humps and hollows to merit archaeological investigation. Medieval deer parks are known elsewhere in Scotland: examples can be seen at Kincardine, near Auchterarder, Cadzow Castle, Hamilton and at Buzzart Dykes in Perthshire.

Whether this is a medieval or post-medieval deer park will perhaps only be answered archaeologically, since no documentary evidence has yet come to light. Similarly, the interior of the park (Steel Park) also contains extensive traces of rig and furrow cultivation **G**, which, together with the possible boundary of the deer park, shows up well on an aerial photograph of the area **figure 3**. If this cultivation is of broad rig type (medieval), it has implications for the dating of the deer park and for the history of settlement at Dalkeith. The practice of emparking often led to the enclosing of land formerly under cultivation, and the eviction of the communities themselves. Important in its own right as a surviving medieval landscape, therefore, the existence of broad rig may also, by association, date the deer park to the medieval period rather than to the seventeenth century.

and regality of Dalkeith with its liberties, with the castle, gardens, orchards, forests and parks, grain and cloth mills, fisheries, rabbit warrens, tenants, coal mines, prebendary and patronage of the collegiate church'. Twenty-two years later, when the same was granted to James, duke of Buccleuch and Monmouth, the lordship was similarly described, but the policies around the castle were specified as 'all the lands included within the stone dyke of the ... park'. Clearly by 1664 the castle was enclosed by a stone wall, but whether it had been so for decades or even centuries before is uncertain.

Equally unclear is whether the original route to the Cow Bridge **F** was more direct than that seen on eighteenth-century maps, the latter following very much the present Musselburgh Road. Cow Bridge was the main crossing over the South Esk and, like the bridge over the North Esk, it needed regular maintenance. There were on-going repairs in the sixteenth and seventeenth centuries and measures, such as taking tolls from those using either the bridge or ford (unspecified), were instituted on a number of occasions.

If one may rely on Blaeu's seventeenth-century plan showing Dalkeith **figure 9**, based much on the work of Timothy Pont who was recording in the late sixteenth century, the route from the town to the South Esk was originally more direct. The artificial bend of Musselburgh Road on eighteenth-century maps, respecting the wall of the Dalkeith Parks and forcing a circuitous route to the bridge, might suggest that the wall was a later feature and that there was originally a more direct route that was later denied by its incorporation into the Dalkeith Parks and the building of a wall. A stray reference to the resignation of a tenement on the south side of the High Street, in 1556, throws an interesting light on this question. The resignation was effected at the green of Dalkeith. According to the evidence of this charter, the green was 'near the castle'. But the topography of the town was such that there was no space for open public ground at the castle end of the High Street. The only available open ground was between where the Duke's Gates now stand and the castle itself. It is possible that here there is evidence of a town green, used by the public, as was the custom in other towns; but which was lost to the ducal policies, perhaps at the time of the extension of the castle in the time of Morton (*see* p 22) or sometime in the seventeenth century. The timing may also coincide with the enclosure of the Steill lands, once cultivated by the burgesses (*see* p 26).

It is known that from the sixteenth century, and probably for many centuries before this, the townspeople were cultivating many acres of land outside the burgh proper. East Acre, for example, which lay to the east of the Cow Bridge, was one such stretch of land, as was the Steill, which stretched to twenty-six acres. Aerial photography reveals the

history

cultivated rigs in the present Steel Park **G**, now enclosed within the Dalkeith estate.

archaeology

There are four bridges over the Esk within the grounds of the house. The Laundry Bridge **C** and Montagu Bridge **D** date to the eighteenth century. Of archaeological interest is the Old Cow Bridge **F**. This is probably medieval in date, and is known to have been repaired in 1594, 1663 and 1685. This bridge lay on the original route from medieval Dalkeith to Musselburgh, before the land was enclosed within the policies of Dalkeith House. Lesslie's map of *c* 1770 **figure 11** shows what may have been the route of this trackway in the gardens as an ornamental feature in a designed landscape. The precise route of this trackway and whether or not its surface was metalled could be determined by archaeological means. The Musselburgh Road almost certainly defines the line of the later road into Dalkeith, after the grounds of the palace were formally enclosed, probably in the seventeenth century.

Apart from the deer park, pathways and an avenue of trees (which lie roughly parallel with the Musselburgh Road), there are few indications of a designed landscape associated with the various phases of the house. Indeed, the elaborate layout depicted on Lesslie's *c* 1770 map does not appear on Wood's map of 1822 **figure 14** some fifty years later, suggesting that the designed landscape may have been planned but never implemented.

figure 24
Fifteenth-century bronze ewer *half size*

archaeology

The chance find of a fifteenth-century bronze ewer **figure 24** was discovered near Dalkeith—outwith the historic core of the town. It measures approximately 21cms in height. The ewer was purchased by the National Museums of Scotland in 1853.

the archaeological potential of Dalkeith a summary **figure 25**

an overview

It is difficult to predict the overall potential for the survival of archaeological deposits within the medieval core of Dalkeith, given the absence of previous archaeological work and chance finds. Nevertheless, routine monitoring and excavations in many other Scottish towns, especially Perth and Aberdeen but also in some smaller burghs, have demonstrated that medieval and later archaeological remains often survive beneath the modern town. The site of any proposed ground disturbance or development along the main street frontages in the historic core of Dalkeith must, therefore, be accorded a high archaeological priority, and arrangements made for the site to be assessed, monitored and, if necessary, excavated in advance of the development scheme. Similarly, any proposed ground disturbance of the surviving streets and wynds themselves (for instance, for essential repairs, access to services, or environmental improvements) should also be monitored routinely, as the remains of important features of the medieval townscape may be sealed beneath them—the market cross, earliest tolbooth, tron, ports and wells—of which no archaeological evidence has yet been found.

To date, there has been no opportunity for archaeological investigation in historic Dalkeith. Thus, the conclusions and recommendations expressed here should be regarded as provisional; this survey will require periodic review in the light of results from any future campaigns of archaeological fieldwork (assessment, monitoring and excavation), and from other types of sub-surface investigations.

It is important to stress that the survey was limited to the core of historic (medieval) Dalkeith, and to Dalkeith House and its immediate environs. Given the wealth of evidence for prehistoric, Roman and early historic remains in the area (*see* pp 12–17), there is a recognised, although unquantifiable, potential for the discovery of archaeological remains of these periods, both within and outwith the confines of the historic burgh. It is important to note that the potential for such discoveries is *not* included in **figure 25**.

Finally, the potential for archaeological features and deposits to be preserved both beneath the floors and within the structures of historic standing buildings in Dalkeith (pp 81–6) must not be forgotten. The archaeological potential of Dalkeith's standing buildings is also *not* shown on **figure 25**, but the potential of individual buildings is considered in the next section.

Turning to the specific areas of Dalkeith (as identified in this survey), documentary and cartographic evidence has demonstrated that all four areas have archaeological potential, with Areas 1 and 3, the core of the medieval town, clearly being the most sensitive to new development. The western limit of the medieval burgh is still uncertain and it is quite possible that early settlement extended into Area 2, perhaps as far as Buccleuch Street. Area 2 incorporates much of the nineteenth-century expansion of the town but also includes isolated sites of interest, such as the mills along the Esk, the origins of which may date from much earlier than the eighteenth century. Area 4 is largely woodland and pasture land, but also contains a number of sites and features of archaeological interest.

figure 25 distinguishes between areas of known archaeological potential (shaded darker green) and unknown potential (shaded lighter green). *All green areas should be treated as potentially archaeologically sensitive. Areas shaded red are Scheduled Ancient Monuments* and are protected by law.

area 1

Situated in the core of the medieval town, Area 1 has high archaeological potential. The street frontage and associated backlands offer the most potential, with archaeological deposits likely to be concentrated in a narrow band along the top of the ridge. At the base of the steep slope down to the river, a broad terrace (Grannies Park) is likely to have proved an attractive location for the numerous mills first recorded in the mid sixteenth century, and has considerable potential for the preservation of industrial archaeology, both medieval and post-medieval.

area 2

The western limit of the medieval town is unclear but settlement may have extended as far as Buccleuch Street. The archaeological potential of Area 2 is likely to be concentrated along the High Street and Buccleuch Street frontages, and their associated backlands. The modern 'Town Centre' overlies much of this, but the lines of the former vennels, and possibly traces of the vennels themselves, have been preserved in the ground plan. Pockets of archaeological deposits may also survive here, below the present standing buildings.

A patchwork of fields lay on the south-west fringes of the town until development pressures began to subsume them in the nineteenth century. Traces of early land divisions and cultivation may still survive within nineteenth-century and more recent housing developments. The sweeping bend in the River South Esk also provided a valuable opportunity to harness the power to run mills, an opportunity not wasted by the inhabitants of Dalkeith. As for the North Esk, the river bank offers high archaeological potential for industrial archaeology, both medieval and post-medieval.

area 3

Area 3 also lies in the core of the medieval town. Archaeological levels here are likely to be concentrated in a band between High Street and St Andrew Street, with the street frontage of High Street, and the former vennels, such as South Street, offering the most archaeological potential. St Andrew Street and its associated frontage may also offer potential for the preservation of the medieval burgage plots (over which they were established) and the activities which took place within them.

Between St Andrew Street and the River South Esk was a patchwork of small fields, and evidence for early cultivation and field boundaries, for example, might survive below present ground level despite the extensive housing schemes now occupying this area. The river bank itself also has archaeological potential; the river would have been an attractive location for industry, such as mills and tanneries, which may have been sited here since the late medieval period.

area 4

The archaeological potential of Area 4 is likely to centre around Dalkeith House, itself a product of centuries of rebuilding; Steel Park, which contains the boundaries of a possibly medieval deer park and broad rig cultivation; and tracts of the grounds, largely woodland, which may mask elements of a former designed landscape. There are also a number of architectural sites and features scattered around the grounds of house, where archaeological observations would be useful in future programmes of refurbishment and restoration. Traces of the earliest (probably twelfth-century) castle might survive in the grounds of Dalkeith House and would be an important archaeological discovery. The early township may also have been located within these grounds. There is also the possibility that the remains of prehistoric sites may survive here.

historic buildings

pp 81–6

D

historic buildings and their archaeological potential

There is much in the historic core of Dalkeith that acts as a reminder of its varied past. Several historic buildings survive, in part or in whole, and although only one is identifiably medieval, these do provide physical clues to Dalkeith's history.

The *church of St Nicholas* **figure 19.A** has a strong visual impact on the townscape **figure 10**. First built in the latter part of the fourteenth century (*see* p 20), it was created a collegiate church in 1405, and underwent considerable change during the next decade. The Reformation, rebuilding, political events of the seventeenth century and major reconstruction in the nineteenth century all had an effect on the church. Only a little remains of the original Gothic building to testify to its early grandeur. This includes the heavily buttressed choir, now badly damaged by weathering, and a few fragments of the nave. In the old choir can still be seen the Morton Monument **figure 7**, with the recumbent effigies of James, first earl of Morton, who died in 1498 and that of his wife, Joanna, daughter of James I. The choir was seen as a testimony to idolatry after the Reformation and was blocked off from the main body of the church, *c* 1590.

Rebuilding of the western portions then commenced, with the church being used as a stable by Cromwell's troops in 1650. The interior was much altered with the addition of lofts to seat the incorporated crafts of the town, particularly in the later seventeenth and eighteenth centuries (*see* pp 32–3). A reminder of these times is the 1665 banner of the Incorporation of Hammermen, still within the church. The Calderwood Monument is sited on the south-west wall, in memory of William Calderwood, minister of Dalkeith from 1659 to 1680. In the sacristy, the Buccleuch family burial vault, with its lead-studded coffins, may still be viewed. Of the early church only a few remnants survive, such as the south porch and the piers in the nave. This is a result of the fact that the parish church, from 1841 known as the East Church (after the construction of the overflow West Church in Old Edinburgh Road), underwent radical recasting and reorientation in 1851–5 by William Burn and David Bryce, including the addition of a west gallery in 1885 and the construction of a new steeple in 1888.

The choir, the only part to avoid restoration in the mid nineteenth century but now becoming increasingly ruinous, is a Scheduled Ancient Monument. Extensions, alterations and restorations over the centuries mean that structural elements of earlier phases of the church, including the original chapel, may be preserved within the present building. Indeed, parts of the south porch and the piers in the nave survive from the original church. Other elements may also have been incorporated into the fabric itself, or may equally survive as foundations sealed below the present floor levels. The position of the church is interesting as is stands slightly skewed in relation to the present alignment of the High Street, and its graveyard almost seems to jut out into the street. Kirkyard boundaries often change, so the possibility that medieval burials might extend out into the street should be considered.

Old Cow Bridge **figure 23.F**, possibly medieval in date and a designated Scheduled Ancient Monument, was on the original routeway from Dalkeith to Musselburgh before it was enclosed within the grounds of Dalkeith House (*see* p 30). It was known to have been repaired in 1594, 1663 and 1685. It comprises a segmental arch of ashlar spanning the river South Esk with a smaller arch over the south bank. The parapets, the eastern of which collapsed in the 1960s, are of brick with stone coping.

While the parish church was the spiritual centre for the burgh community, the market place, market cross, tolbooth and tron were the secular focal points of the town (*see* pp 66–9). Dalkeith's *tolbooth* (176–180 High Street, also designated a Scheduled Ancient Monument) **figures 12 & 21.A**, fronting the widened High Street, the site of the market place (*see* pp 66–9), is a visual reminder of the crucial role that the market held in Dalkeith's past. It was in the tolbooth that market dues were collected and the public weigh-beam was housed. The present building was erected in the late seventeenth century, probably being reworked to some extent in the eighteenth century, and retains many of its original exterior features, although the frontage was probably refaced in the nineteenth century. The whole building underwent refurbishment in 1966. The panel above the doorway, inscribed with the date 1648 and the arms of the earl of Buccleuch, is misleading. It was discovered in the grounds of Dalkeith Palace in the late eighteenth century, and only at that time placed on the tolbooth façade. The tolbooth also functioned as the town's court house, the court room on the first floor having a coffered ceiling. It was here, also, that the town's prison was housed. This consisted of a pit prison in the subterranean basement and an upper prison. Dalkeith's gibbet stood in front of the tolbooth, where the second last public hanging in Scotland took place in 1827.

In other Scottish towns, archaeological excavations have revealed street frontages as the most promising for preservation of archaeological deposits, in spite of the fact that some potential information may have been lost as a result of the building of cellars. The *frontage of Dalkeith High Street* should, therefore, be carefully monitored. Recent excavations in Perth, Dunfermline and Arbroath have also shown that the width and alignment of the main streets in the burghs have changed over the centuries. Earlier cobbled street surfaces and contemporary buildings may be preserved up to three or four metres behind the line of the modern street frontage. This was certainly the case at 80–86 High Street, Perth, where the medieval street lay some four metres further back from the present High Street. At Abbot House, in Dunfermline, recent excavations uncovered a whole section of the medieval street itself inside, and sealed below the floor of, the standing building. Up to six phases of street surfaces were revealed, each separated by thick dumps of midden, containing broken pottery, leather and oyster shells. Here, archaeology clearly demonstrated how dramatically street frontages can shift over time, and the potential for archaeological deposits to be buried below later buildings.

Similarly, buildings which have more than one phase of construction, like the tolbooth, may have earlier structural features sealed within the fabric itself, hidden by later additions. These may be represented by floor surfaces and other features associated with earlier phases of occupation, sealed beneath the modern floor levels, or survive as structural elements.

A scarcely discernible clue to the seventeenth-century past may be seen in the south wall that flanks the entrance from the High Street to the Dalkeith Estate. *Blocked windows and doorways* are the sole reminder of the physical closeness of the homes of townspeople and of their ducal neighbours. They also imply that the wall incorporates the front (or back) walls of now demolished houses; their remains may lie hidden below present ground level.

A number of eighteenth-century buildings survive either partially or totally intact. These offer an insight into the townscape as Dalkeith was emerging as an important market town. *Nos 228–230 High Street* is a three-storey tenement building, typical of the mid eighteenth century, although its original ashlar dressings would have been more prominent before its harling was removed in the 1930s. The pend entrance has a concrete lintel, but otherwise the building retains much of its original character, as a three-bay tenement with an outer stair, now a bay, on its left. On the same side of the street, *nos 216–218 High Street* is a later eighteenth-century house, of two storeys and three bays. Finished in white painted harl, there is an ashlar surround to the door and slightly raised margins to the windows. The raised skews suggest that this house was originally thatched. Further down the High Street, on the same side, modern shop frontages belie the late eighteenth-century origin of *nos 122–126 High Street.* The two upper storeys, however, with their regular windows, reveal the classic style that must have been typical of many houses lining Dalkeith's High Street.

A number of properties on the other side of the High Street also have eighteenth-century origins. *No 41 High Street* has a modern shop frontage at ground level, but retains original features in the two upper floors. *Nos 101 & 103 High Street*, likewise, are three-storeyed and were constructed in the late eighteenth century. Their ground floor frontages are of late nineteenth-century design, but the windows in the upper floors reveal the typical regular fenestration pattern of the late eighteenth century. *Nos 161–163 High Street* is a mid eighteenth-century, L-plan tenement with an asymmetric octagonal stair tower in its north-west angle. It is three-storeyed, with an additional attic, and is reminiscent of the quality buildings that lined the market place in the eighteenth century.

Nos 115 & 117 High Street, with *3–6 Brunton's Close* are interesting eighteenth-century remnants, with later additions and alterations, for example, the nineteenth-century shop windows to the High Street frontage. Not only does the architecture reveal its origins, but the gabled two-storeyed rubble row is a reminder of the earlier street pattern and its associated burgage plots, the row following the original plot lay-out, at right angles to the street. Evidence for the former burgage plots may even lie below the present floor levels. Just nearby, behind the church of St Nicholas are the remnants of *Dalkeith Grammar School* **figure 19.H**, now assimilated into a workshop. This building was put up in the eighteenth century, although the church had long had connections with the grammar school.

Also still respecting the early street pattern is the *Old Meal Market Inn* at 2–4 St Andrew Street **figures 13 & 21.F**. St Andrew Street was originally the back lane to the properties on the south side of High Street, which in its turn developed as Back Street. 2–4 St Andrew Street was built by the owner of a brewery that once stood opposite. The lean-to porch is a replacement for an original external forestair. The adjoining arcaded former cartshed functioned in the nineteenth century as a smithy, although little of its original character now remains. The main dwelling was converted into an inn in 1874.

All the properties along St Andrew Street, despite being *c* 1930s in date, are of potential archaeological interest, as they have been constructed over what had been the backlands of the medieval burgage plots. Evidence of burgage plots can survive buried beneath modern buildings and car parks; and they are an extremely valuable source of information to the urban historian and archaeologist as they often document the activities and conditions of everyday life in a medieval town. Any development in this area should be monitored archaeologically. Excavations in other medieval towns in Scotland, such as Perth, Aberdeen and St Andrews, have revealed middens, rubbish pits, cess pits and vegetable plots as common features of medieval backlands, alongside craft workshops and kilns. A series of three excavations at Canal Street in Perth, for example, showed that the boundaries of these plots were shifted regularly, revealing a fascinating sequence of continually changing plot boundaries, with properties being amalgamated and sub-divided throughout the medieval period.

A group of buildings at *1–3 Musselburgh Road* is a partial remnant of a late eighteenth- or early nineteenth-century larger complex of yards and industrial premises. Although only a two-storey house and outbuildings remain, they are—together with the smithy noted above (*see* p 67), the mills, kiln and skinnery noted below (*see* pp 56, 61 & 66–7), and the ironmills (*see* pp 34 & 62)—a reminder that Dalkeith was dependent on local industry at the turn of the eighteenth and nineteenth centuries, as well as being a market town of growing importance.

Nos 1–5 London Road are an interesting terrace of *c* 1775 houses, with steps directly from the pavement to the front doors. *Nos* 1 and 2 have forestairs to the rear and *no* 3 is more elaborate with a pediment to the street. Originally built as a terrace of three three-bayed houses, *nos* 1–3 were the homes of Dalkeith merchants. Apparently the work of the same group of masons is *no 6 London Road*. Originally constructed in the later eighteenth century as a three-bay house, a fourth bay was later added to its right. Steps, with a wrought iron balustrade, lead up to the central doorway of a panelled door with a two-pane fanlight.

The expanding eighteenth-century townscape is recalled by the remnants of two properties set at some small distance from the historic core of the town. The gate piers of the former Woodburn House, now relocated at *no 37 Woodburn Road*, are in classical style with ashlar urn finials on an ashlar plinth. Although one of the flame finials is missing, they are testimony to the quality of Woodburn House, demolished in 1935, and may have been designed by Robert Adam. At the west end of the town, *Eskbank House* at 14 Glenesk Crescent is almost contemporary with Woodburn House, being constructed in 1794. Built by the minister of Newbattle, Rev James Brown, the house is five-bayed, with two storeys and basement, and steps sweeping up to the main entrance, which has Roman Doric columns, an architrave cornice and a finely detailed radial fanlight. The boundary walls and gate piers are also typical of the quality building of the period in Dalkeith.

Bridges are important features in the long history of Dalkeith, because the town is sited between the North and South Esk rivers. *Newmills Bridge* **figure 21.H** was built in 1756 to afford a crossing over the South Esk. It was widened and repaired in 1812, and largely reconstructed in 1837 and 1839, when three new arches were thrown over it to facilitate movement south. Nearby stands the earlier mill, *Newmills*. Built in 1703, by the mid nineteenth century it formed part of a larger complex, with a mill lade that was blocked by 1892. A change in the masonry colour suggests that the second-floor was a later addition.

Lugton Bridge **figure 19.F** over the North Esk was built nine years after Newmills Bridge and was widened and improved in 1816. There had, however, been a bridge in this vicinity since at least the sixteenth century (*see* p 25). An earlier bridge lay a short distance down river, and is recorded as requiring maintenance in 1594. The exact location of this bridge is uncertain but its foundations may still survive in the river banks. This was an important routeway, leading as it did to Edinburgh. Close by, and dependent on the water source of the North Esk, are three mill buildings. Now forming a mini-industrial estate at Grannies Park, the three were built in the late eighteenth and early nineteenth centuries. The *flour mill* **figure 19.J** is an L-shaped eighteenth-century building of three storeys and a loft, with a later cartshed range. Still visible is the opening to the arched mill race. Beside this, the five-bay *mill building* has a first-floor granary loft breaking through the eaves and there is evidence on the masonry to the eastern elevation of a now disappeared kiln. A two-storeyed block, it is seen as single storeyed at street level. The six-bay *mill building* is early nineteenth century in date. There is a forestair to the south-east corner and the building curves to follow the line of the road. Closely associated with these three is a former *skinnery*. A late eighteenth-century building, it was heightened in the nineteenth century. In the mid nineteenth century there was a forestair on the western elevation. Mills are recorded as early as the 1540s in Dalkeith, the sweeping bend in the River North Esk providing an ideal opportunity to draw water to power the mills and return it to its original source. Mills were often converted from one process to another as the economy dictated. As a result, many have been shown to have incorporated earlier structures. The origins of the mills that survive along this stretch of the river may, therefore, go much further back in time than the external structures would suggest.

On the other side of the North Esk, *nos 2–8 Bridgend* is a row of attractive dwellings, facing the North Esk. *No* 6 may incorporate some eighteenth-century remnants, but is predominantly early nineteenth century, with an octagonal stair tower. *No* 8 is, likewise, early nineteenth century in origin. *Nos* 2 and 4 are dateable to the late eighteenth century, *no* 2 being the earlier.

In quite different character, but also built in the eighteenth century, is *Dalkeith House* **figure 23.A**. Although not technically within the burgh, the presence of the castle, later converted into a palace, and its occupants and visitors had a profound effect on the town and its life (*passim*). The first fortified building here was possibly constructed in the twelfth century. Documentary references to great depths of top soil suggest that this earliest castle was of motte and bailey type, and would have comprised an earthen, flat-topped mound, topped by a wooden tower. A palisade around the top edge of the mound provided extra defence. An outer, defensive ditch would have surrounded the base of the mound, the upcast from which formed the fabric of the motte itself. Mottes often have an outer enclosure, or bailey. This contained many of the domestic buildings and structures, and it was only during an attack that the tower on the motte itself was occupied. If a motte existed here, then it may later have been converted to a stone castle, by the replacement of existing timber defences in stone. Within a stone curtain wall, a range of buildings, probably of timber, would have stood around an open central courtyard. It would be natural that a readily defensible spot would attract settlers to cluster near it for protection. The castle would also need supplies and manpower and this, in turn, would have attracted nearby settlement. It is, therefore, highly probable that the site of the earliest settlement lies in the present estate of Dalkeith.

The owners of Dalkeith Castle **figure 6**, the Douglas family, who from 1457 were the earls of Morton, were of sufficient importance on the political scene that the township was to participate in many national events, some welcome and others disastrous for the peace of the settlement. There is evidence, for example, that Dalkeith was sacked and burned on many occasions in the medieval period and in the sixteenth century (*see* pp 21 & 23). The castle, however, was of sufficient grandeur by this time that it was often host to royalty. The presence of nobility and royal retinue would not only have been a common sight in the town, but would also have provided employment and a market for supplies.

In the 1570s James Douglas, fourth earl of Morton, converted the castle into a Scottish Renaissance palace, known locally as the 'Lion's Den', so feared was he **figure 8**. In 1642, it was sold to the earls of Buccleuch; and from 1654 to 1659 it was the residence of General Monck. Anne, duchess of Buccleuch, returned from England sometime around 1701 and immediately set about upgrading the family home. James Smith was commissioned to design and effect the alterations. This new eighteenth-century palace incorporated a number of the features of Morton's original. The south-eastern courtyard wall was demolished, parts of the earlier building were absorbed, particularly in the south-western corner and probably also in the north and west wings. This U-plan mansion had one of the earliest classical façades in Scotland. The lavishness of the interior and the trappings that accompanied it were of equal grandeur. Repair and refacing by John Adam took place in 1762–3; and it is possible that some of the detailed richness comes from this time. Later in the century, in the 1780s, a few alterations were effected, including the addition of a bow-fronted library in the east range, by William Playfair. Further modifications were effected in 1831 by William Burn, although most of his original design was not adopted.

Dalkeith House, as it stands today, is the product of centuries of building, alterations and refurbishments, all of which survive in some form or another. Structural elements of all of the earlier phases may be contained, or even incorporated, within the fabric of the present building or lie sealed below the present floor levels. As the later conversion of the palace to country house absorbed much of the existing standing building, the very earliest phases may be the most archaeologically testing. At its core is an early castle, dating very probably to the twelfth century. The conversion of the palace to country house involved the demolition of the south-east courtyard wall. This is likely to have had fairly substantial foundations and should survive below present ground level.

Other features in Dalkeith Park still stand as testament to the grandeur and importance of the house of Buccleuch. The *stables* and coach-house, designed by William Adam, were erected in 1740. The complex could accommodate about sixty horses, carriages and the staff required to work them. Nearby are the eighteenth-century (or possibly early nineteenth-century) classical *laundry* and *laundry bridge. Montagu Bridge* **figure 23.D**, spanning the North Esk, was designed by Robert Adam and constructed by his brother James in 1792. Three huge life-sized sculptures of stags were originally prominent features along the bridge parapet, but these were removed as they frightened the horses. The bridge was erected by the third duke to celebrate the inheritance by his wife of the Montagu estates. The remnants of a magnificent *conservatory* **figure 23.E** still stand, near to the stable block. It was built *c* 1832 to a design of William Burn. Used to grow mediterranean-type fruits, such as oranges and figs, its cavernous basement housed a boiler which heated the glass structure.

The gateway to the estate from the High Street, the *Duke's Gates* **figure 21.C**, was erected in 1784 by James Playfair. The four square piers are linked by a screen wall, with the gateway of cast iron, with leaf design, at the centre. They form an imposing definition of separateness of estate and town, notwithstanding the close links forged over the centuries. Just beside them stands the later, simple *lodge house. St Mary's Episcopal Church* stands inside the gates. Built about 1835, as the Buccleuch family's private chapel, to a design of William Burn and David Bryce, the church houses a unique hydraulic organ and bell-ringing mechanism. The magnificent interior, with Minton tile floors and superb stained glass windows, is a reminder of the wealth and status of the Buccleuch family in the nineteenth century. The chapel was transferred to the congregation in 1958.

In spite of major development of the town centre in the twentieth century, there is visual evidence throughout the town of Dalkeith's nineteenth-century prosperity, in the form of dwellings, shop frontages, public houses and bank buildings. Detailed information about these buildings may be gained from: Historic Scotland's 'Statutory List of Listed Buildings'; C McWilliam's *Lothian, except Edinburgh* (Edinburgh, 1978—in *The Buildings of Scotland* series); and from J Thomas, *Midlothian, An Illustrated Architectural Guide* (Edinburgh, 1995). A number of key nineteenth-century standing buildings have strong statements to make about Dalkeith's historic past. The overview below is not comprehensive and fuller information may be gained from the above publications. It must also be remembered that nineteenth-century buildings may also incorporate earlier structures. Buildings of any date situated in the core of the medieval burgh were almost certainly constructed on the site of, or directly over, earlier buildings, a sequence possibly going back to the medieval period and continuing up to the present day. Although there has been no opportunity to examine any of the street frontages in Dalkeith, evidence of earlier, possibly medieval structures may be expected to survive, sealed beneath eighteenth- or nineteenth-century standing buildings within the medieval core of the town, and particularly along the High Street and the vennels leading off it.

The *Cross Keys Hotel* at 182 High Street was a smart coaching inn, built *c* 1804 and used frequently by those travelling from Edinburgh south to the Borders, Carlisle and London, and back again. The carriage pend to the right may still be seen and the tripartite Doric-pilastered doorpiece gives access to the ground floor, which leads via a cast-iron balustraded stair to the first floor function room, which runs the full length of the building.

Nearby, at 200 High Street, stands the once impressive *Corn Exchange* **figure 16**. Built by public subscription, it was the biggest indoor grain market in Scotland. Twin gabled, in Jacobean style, it has a hood-moulded entrance. The gableheads are surmounted with ball finials and weathervanes. The high open hall inside has a double-hammerbeam roof and a gallery to its west. Although now somewhat dilapidated, it is a fine encapsulation of Dalkeith's nineteenth-century status.

Across the road at 175 High Street stands *Militia House*, so called as it apparently housed the Duke of Buccleuch's small private regiment, the 'Duke's Canaries'; and later, *c* 1864, served to accommodate officers when barracks were built at what is now Elmfield Court. The two-storeyed rectangular house is the remaining portion of an L-shaped residence, which had a rendered stair tower (still standing) in its re-entrant angle. Next door, at 177 High Street, is *Dalkeith Park House*. Built *c* 1830 to a design of William Burn, it was constructed for the Duke of Buccleuch's chamberlain, to replace the dwelling which originally stood within the gates of Dalkeith Palace. It was the chamberlain's role to conduct Dalkeith's affairs until it became a police burgh in 1878. In baronial style, it is composed of two storeys, with a single-storeyed wing linking to the stable and coach-house range.

The *Ironmills* in Ironmills Park is a reminder of Dalkeith's connection with ironmilling since at least 1648. The water-powered mill produced various iron goods, including clogs for miners. The power came from a weir on the River North Esk to the west, but the mill lade has been infilled since 1963. Still standing in the complex are the mill itself, a linking wing, the millers' dwelling house and a cartshed range.

Another interesting architectural feature is the *Watch Tower* **figure 20.F** in the burial ground on Old Edinburgh Road. Built in the early decades of the nineteenth century by the Committee of Dalkeith Churchyard Association, its purpose was to house overnight armed watchmen, who guarded the graveyard from body snatchers. Nearby stands the *West Church* **figure 20.E**. Built in 1840 to a design of William Burn, it is indicative of the growing population of the town in the nineteenth century. The growing congregation in the parish church of St Nicholas had put pressure on the inadequate accommodation, and so the fifth duke of Buccleuch gifted the site and built and endowed the church.

Further to the west is *Dalkeith Water Tower*. One of the first actions of Dalkeith town council, founded in 1878, was to come to terms with the town's ongoing problem of inadequate supply of clean water. A year later, the pagoda-style tower was erected to hold the supply for Eskbank. By this time, the town had expanded westwards along Eskbank Road, as may still be appreciated by the number of nineteenth-century villas still standing in this area.

historical research objectives

Little is known of the first urban settlement at Dalkeith. Much of the early documentation refers merely to the lordship and barony of Dalkeith, but this is an area which would merit more extensive documentary research.

The resource material for the late medieval and the early modern period is extensive and it was not possible to study all of this in depth in the time available. Kirk session records, for example, with fuller details of Dalkeith witch trials, should provide a fruitful basis for further research. Justiciary court records, the first of which dates from 1516, were not used for this survey, but they will throw incidental light on the society and lifestyle of sixteenth-century Dalkeith. Private documentation, such as the Morton Papers, now in the care of the Scottish Record Office, should be assessed more fully.

Perhaps the most extensive source for the history of Dalkeith is the Buccleuch Muniments (SRO GD 224). Whilst these have provided an invaluable insight into seventeenth- and eighteenth-century Dalkeith, large parts of this resource would merit closer study.

The nineteenth century has been largely neglected in this Survey, also due to the constraints of time. There is a wide variety of primary documentation available for this period, perhaps the most interesting being the unusual early run of census data (SRO CH2/84/41–7). The extent of these records, alone, would justify fuller research.

archaeological objectives for the future

Preparation of the Dalkeith burgh survey has highlighted a number of directions for future archaeological work. These can be broadly divided into management objectives, priorities for future fieldwork, and other areas which merit further research. Any such list cannot be exhaustive but it should cover the main areas of concern in the foreseeable future.

management objectives

1 Wherever possible, it is important to monitor the impact of any development (in its broadest sense) on the potential archaeological resource (the **light and dark green areas** on **figure 25**). This will require the routine provision of site-specific desk-based assessments, through to watching briefs, trial excavations and, where necessary, controlled excavation, post-excavation analysis and publication. Over time, the cumulative results will 'calibrate' this assessment of the archaeological potential of the burgh, providing evidence about the burgh's origins, and its physical, economic and social development through the centuries.

2 Developments should similarly be monitored to shed more light on the prehistory of Dalkeith, particularly in the Roman and later prehistoric period.

3 The degree and nature of cellarage along the main streets were not systematically examined during the preparation of this report. More accurate information would be most useful to managers/curators of the archaeological resource in assessing the archaeological potential of these and other main street frontages in the burgh.

4 Engineers' boreholes offer a convenient glimpse of the depth and nature of sub-surface deposits, man-made or not, ancient and modern. It would be useful if the results obtained from engineers' boreholes in and around the core of the historic burgh could be gradually collected and collated. Borehole results, especially those in the hands of private contractors, have proved difficult to access, and it might be worth considering mechanisms by which such information could more easily (and preferably routinely) be made available to managers/curators of the archaeological resource.

5 Opportunities should continue to be taken to increase public awareness of the potential archaeological interest of Dalkeith, both generally and within and beneath historic standing buildings.

6 Periodic review and updating of this survey would be desirable to take account of the results of any future archaeological work, and of the comprehensive collection and collation of other types of sub-surface investigations, such as engineers' bore holes, systematic survey of cellarage on the main street frontages *etc*. In particular, the colour-coded map **figure 25** should be revised and re-issued at regular intervals.

priorities for future fieldwork

As no archaeological investigations have so far been undertaken in Dalkeith, the priorities for future archaeological fieldwork are fairly rudimentary. However, the following priorities should be borne in mind during preparations of future project designs:

1 Recover any evidence of the structural history of Dalkeith House, from possible motte and bailey through to country house.

2 Ascertain whether a settlement developed around the early castle.

3 Establish a date for the construction of the possible deer park. The structural details of one surviving stretch of the park pale suggest it may be medieval in origin, but with a later retaining wall built into the inner face of the perimeter bank.

4 Confirm that the extensive rig and furrow identified within the possible deer park is of broad rig type (medieval), and determine its relationship to the boundaries of the deer park. This may establish that the land had been cleared prior to enclosure, perhaps shifting the focus of settlement to present-day Dalkeith.

5 Define the limits of the medieval burgh and the character and date of any burgh boundaries.

6 Establish the date and nature of the early chapel of St Nicholas, and its subsequent development. A *maison dieu* is known to have stood nearby, but the exact location is unknown.

archaeology

7 Locate the important features of the medieval townscape—the earliest tolbooth, market cross, tron, ports and wells, for example—of which no archaeological evidence has yet been found.

8 Identify the medieval routeway into Dalkeith from Musselburgh. This was known to have crossed the South Esk at the Old Cow Bridge, from which point it must have crossed land later enclosed within the grounds of the palace.

9 Recover evidence for medieval industries. The numerous eighteenth-century mills located along the River North Esk, for example, may have been built directly over, or incorporated, late medieval mills. The standing mills also merit further study.

10 Identify any sequence of planning in the lay-out and expansion of the burgh, and determine any variation in street alignment and width.

11 Assess the nature of the burgage plots in the burgh and define what medieval activities were taking place within them.

12 Ascertain the nature of outlying settlements such as those at Bridgend and Newmills.

13 Recover any evidence of a designed landscape at Dalkeith House.

areas for further archaeological research

1 A survey of the possible deer park and the rig and furrow identified within it would provide a rare and valuable opportunity to gain an understanding of what appears to be a surviving medieval landscape, on the very edge of a medieval town. It would also establish the relationship between the cultivation of this land and the establishment of the deer park, which may have implications for the origins of settlement at Dalkeith.

2 In due course, reconstruction of the lay-out, extent and physical setting of the medieval burgh may be possible and would benefit our understanding of its development through the centuries. This would be particularly useful when assessing the impact of any proposed future developments and in presenting the current state of knowledge.

street names

pp 91–93

D

Buccleuch Street

Area 2

Dalkeith passed to the Buccleuchs in the mid seventeenth century. The estate was purchased in 1642 by Francis, second earl of Buccleuch, who passed it on to his elder daughter, Mary, and then his younger daughter, Anne, and her husband, the Duke of Monmouth (the illegitimate son of Charles II). They were created Duke and Duchess of Buccleuch in 1663. It was Duchess Anne who, after her husband's execution in 1685, commissioned the rebuilding (restyling) of Dalkeith Palace into what is more or less Dalkeith House as it stands today. The present ninth duke of Buccleuch and eleventh duke of Queensberry still owns the house, but currently leases it to an American university. The family seat is at Bowhill in Selkirkshire.

Croft Street

Area 2

Croft Street more or less marked the western limit of the town in the mid nineteenth century and was presumably so named because crofts lay beyond it. East of Croft Street are the properties that extended back from the Buccleuch Street frontage, including some quite sizeable villas.

Duke Street

Area 3

This street name no doubt commemorates the dukes of Buccleuch, whose interests in Dalkeith date back to mid seventeenth century, when the earls of Buccleuch purchased the estate. Duke Street appears to have been created out of two narrow vennels that provided access between the medieval burgage plots, from High Street to Back Lane which ran behind the plots (now St Andrew Street).

Edinburgh Road

Areas 1 & 2

This is a late addition to the town plan, designed to provide a more direct access into the town centre. Originally named New Road, and shown on John Wood's 1822 plan and the 1853 Ordnance Survey plan of the town, it was later renamed Edinburgh Road.

Eskbank Road

Area 2

Eskbank Road, taking its name from the river, is essentially a continuation of Dalkeith's High Street, running south-west to Eskbank, now virtually a suburb of Dalkeith.

Glebe Street

Area 2

Glebe Street is named after the glebe fields that stood on either side of the Old Edinburgh Road. The glebe fields were lands from which the minister of the parish church could obtain an income.

High Street

Areas 1, 2 & 3

High Street was the name given to the main thoroughfare in most medieval Scottish towns and Dalkeith was no exception. This was the commercial centre of the town where the market was located and the other typical features of the medieval townscape, such as the market cross, tolbooth and tron stood.

Ironmills Road

Area 2
Ironmills Road is a modern street which runs along the southern bank of the River North Esk. This area was home to a number of mills, including a waulk mill and a barley mill. Slightly further west, however, is a water-powered iron mill which stands today in the park of the same name. The standing buildings are nineteenth century in date but iron milling is recorded in Dalkeith as early as the mid seventeenth century.

London Road

Area 2
London Road is one of the main roads south in Scotland. Elsewhere, the same road is known as Buccleuch Street and Newmills Road. South-east of Dalkeith, this road is known as Lauder Road.

Lothian Street

Area 2
Lothian Street is essentially the southern end of South Street, before it continues on to Newbattle as Abbey Road. At the northern end of Lothian Street, at its junction with South Street, was the nineteenth-century cattle market.

Mitchell Street

Area 2
This street was developed in the twentieth century and may have been named after a partner in Sydney Mitchell and Wilson, a firm of architects. They worked in Dalkeith and designed the Commercial Bank (*nos* 7–9) in Eskbank Road.

Musselburgh Road

Area 3
This street may have developed from one of the numerous vennels or closes which provided access between the medieval burgage plots. In the nineteenth century, at least, it was known as Chapel Street and is marked as such on Wood's plan of 1822. It was possibly named after the United Presbyterian Church which stood on the west corner of High Street and Chapel Street. The wheat, barley and pease market also stood here in the early nineteenth century. It was later renamed Musselburgh Road and is now one of the main routes (the A6094) out of Dalkeith to the coast, skirting around the walled grounds of Dalkeith House.

Newmills Road

Area 3
This is effectively the A68 which cuts through the town, and is elsewhere known as London Road, Buccleuch Street and Old Edinburgh Road.

North Wynd

Area 2
North Wynd, which lay to the north of the High Street, no longer exists, since it was demolished in 1936 prior to the construction of a new housing development.

Old Edinburgh Road

Area 2
This was the original road from Edinburgh and the north into Dalkeith, crossing over the River North Esk at Lugton Bridge. In the early nineteenth century, a more direct access was constructed—first named New Street, then renamed Edinburgh Road.

St Andrew Street

Area 3
St Andrew Street was developed as a street frontage in the 1930s, over what had been a long established back lane (Back Lane) behind the original medieval burgage plots. It was during this phase of development that many of the narrow vennels which provided access between the burgage plots were demolished.

South Street

Area 2
This street developed from a narrow vennel which ran south off the High Street, called the Common Vennel. By the early nineteenth century, it was being referred to as South Street, as shown on Wood's 1822 plan of the town, but only a few years later, on the 1853 Ordnance Survey plan of the town, it was named High Street South. It presently carries much of the traffic through the town.

West Wynd

Area 2
West Wynd has, like many of the old vennels in the town, disappeared, in this case to make way for the 'Town Centre' shopping mall. The lines of the former streets and vennels have, however, been largely preserved in the ground plan of the mall.

glossary

pp 95–7

D

glossary

adze	A cutting tool.
auxiliary fort	Housed the *auxilia*, comprised of units of infantry and of cavalry with a nominal strength of 500 or 1000 men.
annexe	An area adjacent to the main Roman fort.
backlands	The area to the rear of the burgage plot behind the dwelling house on the frontage. Originally intended for growing produce and keeping animals; site of wells and midden heaps. Eventually housed working premises of craftsmen and poorer members of burgh society.
bailies	Burgh officer-bearers who performed routine administration.
barrow	An artificial earth mound.
baxters	Bakers.
beakers	A distinctive type of Bronze Age pottery.
boundaries	*see* burgage plot
burgage plot	A division of land, often of regular size, having been measured out by liners, allocated to a burgess. Once built on, it contained the burgage house on the frontage (*see* frontage) and a backland (*see* backland). In time, with pressure for space, the plots were often subdivided, a process known as repletion. Plots were bounded by ditches, wattle fences or stone walls.
burgess	Person who enjoys the privileges and responsibilities of the freedom of the burgh.
cairn	Mound of stones, often covering Bronze Age burials.
cinerary urns	A form of burial dating to the Bronze Age, whereby the cremated remains were placed in urns.
cists	Stone-lined graves.
close	*see* vennel
collegiate church	A church with an endowment of a continuing community of secular clergy. The presiding cleric normally held the title of provost.
craft	Trade.
cropmark	Crops which grow over buried archaeological sites ripen at differing rates and show up as marks on aerial photographs.
denarius	A type of Roman coin.
documentary sources	Written evidence, primary sources being the original documents.

ewer	A pitcher or water jug.
façade	The finished face of a building.
Flavian	A period in Roman history, dating to the late first century AD.
frontage	Front part of burgage plot nearest the street, on which the dwelling was usually built.
gap sites	Burgage plots not built up or 'biggit'; in a modern context, undeveloped space between two buildings.
henge	A Bronze Age ritual enclosure.
hinterland	Rural area around a burgh, to which the burgh looked for economic and agricultural support; hinterland likewise dependent on burgh market.
hoard	A collection of material deposited in the ground, often buried for safe-keeping but never recovered.
igneous rock	Rock produced by volcanic agency.
Improvement	Period beginning in the eighteenth century when land was improved and enclosed.
indwellers	Unprivileged, non-burgess dwellers in a town.
inhumation	A burial of an uncremated body.
intervallum	An open area around the inside of the defensive rampart of a Roman fort.
marching camp	Often called temporary camps, these were constructed each night by the Roman army on military campaigns.
midden	Rubbish heaps consisting of mainly food debris and other waste products, often found in the backlands of medieval properties.
palisade	Timber fence intended for defence.
patera	A bronze saucepan.
pit alignment	A prehistoric land boundary.
prehistory	Period of the human past before the advent of writing.
rampart	An artificial earthen or stone bank.
repletion	*see* burgage plot
rig	*see* burgage plot
steelyard	A weigh-beam.

tectonic movements	Displacements in the earth's crust.
titulum	A short length of traverse-rampart and ditch protecting the gateway of a Roman camp.
toft	*see* burgage plot
tolbooth	The most important secular building; meeting place of burgh council; collection post for market tolls; often housed town gaol.
tolls	Payments for use of burgh market.
tron	Public weigh-beam.
vennel	Alley; narrow lane.
£	£ Scots.

bibliography

pp 99–103

D

Scottish Record Office
B52/3/3 Musselburgh Council Minute Book, 1762–1786.
CH2/424/1 Register of the Presbytery of Dalkeith, 1582–1630.
CH2/84/41–7 Dalkeith Census Data.
EH69/16/1 Hearth Tax, Midlothian.
GD1 Miscellaneous Accessions.
GD18 Clerk of Penicuik Collection.
GD26 Inventory of Leven and Melville Muniments.
GD40 Lothian Muniments.
GD103 Antiquaries Charters (Livingstone).
GD150 The Morton Papers.
GD224 The Buccleuch Muniments.
GD406 Hamilton Muniments.
RH11 Dalkeith Justiciary Court Book, 1516.

Kilmarnock District Council
MS 1/1/1

printed primary sources

Accounts of the Lord High Treasurer of Scotland, 13 vols, edd T Dickson *et al* (Edinburgh, 1877–).
Accounts of the Masters of Works for Building and Repairing Royal Palaces and Castles, 2 vols, edd H M Paton *et al* (Edinburgh, 1957–82).
The Acts of the Lords Auditors of Causes and Complaints, ed T Thomson (London, 1839).
The Acts of the Lords of Council in Public Affairs, 1501–1554, ed R K Hannay (Edinburgh, 1932).
The Acts of the Parliaments of Scotland, 12 vols, edd T Thomson *et al* (Edinburgh, 1814–75).
Adam, R (ed), *City of Edinburgh Old Accounts, 1544–1567*, 2 vols (Edinburgh, 1899).
Anderson, A O (ed), *Early Sources of Scottish History, 500–1286*, 2 vols (Edinburgh, 1922).
Anderson, J (ed), *The Laing Charters 854–1837* (Edinburgh, 1899).
Bain, J *et al* (edd), *Calendar of Documents relating to Scotland*, 5 vols (Edinburgh, 1881–1969).
Balfour-Melville, E W M (ed), *An Account of the Proceedings of the Estates of Scotland, 1689–1690*, 2 vols (SHS, 1954–5).
Balfour-Paul, J (ed), *The Scots Peerage*, 9 vols (Edinburgh, 1904–14).
Blaikie, W B (ed), *Itinerary of Prince Charles Edward Stewart* (SHS, 1897).
Calderwood, D, *History of the Kirk of Scotland*, 8 vols (Woodrow Society, 1842–9).
Calendar of Documents Relating to Scotland, 5 vols, edd J Bain et al (Edinburgh 1881–1969).
Calendar of State Papers relating to Scotland and Mary, Queen of Scots, 13 vols, edd J Bain *et al* (Edinburgh 1898–1967).
Clark, J T (ed), *MacFarlane's Genealogical Collections* (SHS, 1900).
Constable, A (trans), *John Major's Greater Britain* (SHS, 1892).
Cowan, I B & Easson, D E, *Medieval Religious Houses: Scotland* (London, 1976).
Dawson, J H, *Statistical History of Scotland* (Edinburgh, 1855).
Defoe, D, *A Tour through the Whole Island of Great Britain, 1724*, abridged edition, edd P N Furbank & W R Owens (New Haven, 1991).
Donaldson, G (ed), *Thirds of Benefices, 1561–1572* (SHS, 1949).
Dunlop, A I (ed), *Calendar of Scottish Supplications to Rome, 1423–1428* (SHS, 1956).
The Exchequer Rolls of Scotland, edd J Stuart *et al*, 23 vols (Edinburgh, 1878–).
Fasti Ecclesiae Scoticanae, ed H Scott, 10 vols (Edinburgh, 1915–1981).
Firth, C H (ed), *Scotland and the Commonwealth* (SHS, 1895).
Firth, C H (ed), *Scotland and the Protectorate* (SHS, 1899).
Fraser, W (ed), *The Lennox*, 2 vols (Edinburgh, 1874).
Fraser, W (ed), *The Scotts of Buccleuch*, 2 vols (Edinburgh, 1878).

Fraser, W (ed), *The Douglas Book*, 4 vols (Edinburgh, 1885).
Gray, J (ed), *Clerk of Penicuik's Memoirs, 1676–1755* (SHS, 1892).
Gray, J (ed), *Scottish Population Statistics* (SHS, 1952).
Groome, F H, *Ordnance Gazetteer of Scotland: A Survey of Scottish Topography*, 6 vols (Edinburgh, 1886).
Hamilton Papers: Letters and Papers Illustrating the Political Relations of England and Scotland in the Sixteenth Century, ed J Bain, 2 vols (Edinburgh, 1892).
Hannay, R K (ed), *Rentale Sancti Andree, 1538–1546* (SHS, 1913).
Heron, R, *Scotland Delineated* (Edinburgh, 1799).
Hume Brown, P (ed), *Early Travellers in Scotland* (Edinburgh, 1891).
Innes, C (ed), *Liber Sancte Marie de Melros*, 2 vols (Bannatyne Club, 1837).
Innes, C (ed), *Liber Cartarum Sancte Crucis* (Bannatyne Club, 1840).
Innes, C (ed), *Registrum Sancte Marie de Neubotle* (Bannatyne Club, 1849).
Innes, C (ed), *Origines Parochiales*, 2 vols (Edinburgh, 1854).
Kirk, J (ed), *The Books of Assumption of the Thirds of Benefices. Scottish Ecclesiastical Rentals at the Reformation* (Oxford, 1995).
Kyd, J G (ed), *Scottish Population Statistics, including Webster's Analysis of Population, 1755* (SHS, 1952).
Laing, D (ed), *The Bannatyne Miscellany, ii*, (Bannatyne Club, 1836).
Laing, D (ed), *Registrum domus de Soltre, necnon Ecclesie Collegiate S. Trinitatis prope Edinburgh* (Bannatyne Club, 1861).
Lewis, S, *A Topographical Dictionary of Scotland*, 2 vols (London, 1843–6).
MacFarlane, W, *Geographical Collections Relating to Scotland*, 3 vols, ed A Mitchell (SHS, 1906–08).
McLeod, W (ed) *A List of Persons concerned in the Rebellion 1745–1746* (SHS, 1890).
Marwick, J (ed), *Extracts from the Records of the Convention of Royal Burghs of Scotland*, 7 vols, (Edinburgh, 1870–1918).
Marwick, J (ed), *Miscellany of the Scottish Burgh Records Society* (SBRS, 1881).
Marwick, J D *et al* (edd), *Extracts from the Records of the Burgh of Edinburgh*, 11 vols (SBRS, 1871–1967).
The New Statistical Account of Scotland, 14 vols (Edinburgh, 1845); vol i, Edinburgh, ed Committee of the Society for the Benefit of the Sons and Daughters of the Clergy.
Pennant, T, *A Tour of Scotland MDCCLXIX*, 3rd edition, ed B Knight (Perth, 1979).
Pococke, R, *Tours in Scotland: 1747, 1750, 1760*, ed D W Kemp (SHS, 1887).
Pryde, G S (ed), *The Burghs of Scotland: A Critical List* (Oxford, 1965).
Regesta Regum Scottorum:
vol i *The Acts of Malcolm IV, King of Scots, 1153–1165,* ed G W S Barrow (Edinburgh, 1960).
vol v *The Acts of Robert I, King of Scots, 1306–1329,* ed A A M Duncan (Edinburgh, 1988).
vol vi *The Acts of David II, King of Scots, 1329–1371,* ed B Webster (Edinburgh, 1982).
Rogers, C (ed), *Social Life in Scotland* (Grampian Club, 1886).
Sanford Terry, C (ed), *The Cromwellian Union* (SHS, 1902).
Simpson, G G (ed), *Scottish Handwriting 1150–1650*, (Aberdeen, 1986).
Spottiswoode, J, *History of the Church of Scotland*, 3 vols (Edinburgh, 1845–51).
The Register of the Great Seal of Scotland, 11 vols, edd J M Thomson *et al* (Edinburgh, 1882–1914).
The Register of the Privy Council of Scotland, edd J H Burton *et al*
First Series, 14 vols (Edinburgh, 1877–98)
Second Series, 8 vols (Edinburgh, 1899–1908)
Third Series, 16 vols (Edinburgh, 1908–).
The Register of the Privy Seal of Scotland (Registrum Secreti Sigilli Regum Scotorum), 8 vols, edd M Livingstone *et al* (Edinburgh, 1908–).
The Statistical Account of Scotland 1791–9, vol ii, *The Lothians*, ed J Sinclair. New Edition, edd D J Withrington & I R Grant (Wakefield, 1978).

The Third Statistical Account, Midlothian, ed H Kirkland (Edinburgh, 1985).
Thomson, T (ed), *Acts and Proceedings of the General Assemblies of the Kirk of Scotland, from the year MDLX*, 3 vols (Bannatyne Club, 1839–45).
Thomson, T (ed), *A Diary of the Public Correspondence of Sir Thomas Hope of Craighall, Bart, 1633–1645* (Bannatyne Club, 1843).
Thomson, T *et al* (edd), *Registrum Honoris de Morton*, 2 vols (Bannatyne Club, 1853).
Watt, D E R, *Fasti Ecclesiae Scoticanae Medii Aevi ad Annum 1638* (SRS, 1969).
Wilson, J M (ed), *The Imperial Gazetteer of Scotland* (Edinburgh, n.d.).

secondary sources

Baldwin, J R, *Exploring Scotland's Heritage: Lothian and the Borders* (Edinburgh, 1985).
Barber, J, 'The Pit Alignment at Eskbank Nurseries', *Proceedings of the Prehistoric Society*, 51 (1985), 149–66.
Breeze, D J, *Roman Scotland: frontier country* (London, 1996).
Brown, C J & Shipley, B M, *Soil Survey of Scotland: South East Scotland. Soil and Land Capability for Agriculture* (The Macaulay Institute for Soil Research, Aberdeen, 1982).
Burton, J H, *History of Scotland*, 8 vols (Edinburgh, 1874).
Cameron, I B & Stephenson, D *The Midland Valley of Scotland* (British Regional Geology, 3rd edn, London, 1985).
Campbell, R H, *Scotland since 1707* (Oxford, 1971).
Carrick, J C, *Around Dalkeith and Camp Meg* (Leicester, 1984).
Chalmers, G, *Caledonia*, 8 vols (Paisley, 1887–1902).
Darvill, T, *Prehistoric Britain* (London, 1987).
Dennison, E P & Coleman, R, *Historic Musselburgh: The Archaeological Implications of Development* (Scottish Burgh Survey, 1996).
Dickson, J, *The Ruined Castles of Midlothian* (Edinburgh, 1894).
Donald, P, *An Uncounselled King* (Cambridge, 1990).
Donaldson, G, *Scotland: James V to James VII* (Edinburgh, 1987).
Dow, F D, *Cromwellian Scotland* (Edinburgh, 1979).
Dunbar, J G, *The Historic Architecture of Scotland* (London, 1966).
Duncan, A A M, *Scotland: the Making of the Kingdom* (Edinburgh, 1975).
Edmonds, E, *The Geological Map: an Anatomy of the Landscape* (HMSO, London, 1983).
Eyre-Todd, G, *Famous Scottish Burghs* (London, 1923).
Feacham, R, *Guide to Prehistoric Scotland* (London, 1977).
Ferguson, D, *Six Centuries in and around the Church of St Nicholas* (Glasgow, 1951).
Ferguson, D, *The Collegiate Church of St Nicholas* (no place, 1963).
Ferguson, W, *Scotland: 1689 to the Present* (Edinburgh, 1987).
Furgol, E M, *A Regimental History of the Covenanting Armies* (Edinburgh, 1990).
Gilbert, J M, *Hunting and Hunting Reserves in Medieval Scotland* (Edinburgh, 1979).
Hanson, W S, *Agricola and the Conquest of the North* (London, 1987).
Hanson, W S & Breeze, D J, 'The Future of Roman Scotland', in W S Hanson & E A Salter (edd), *Scottish Archaeology: New Perspectives* (Aberdeen, 1991).
Hanson, W S & Maxwell, G, *Rome's North West Frontier. The Antonine Wall* (Edinburgh, 1983).
Hume Brown, P, *History of Scotland*, 3 vols (Cambridge, 1912).
Keay, J & Keay, J (edd), *Collins Encyclopaedia of Scotland* (London, 1994).
Keppie, L, *Scotland's Roman Remains* (Edinburgh, 1986).
Lang, A, *History of Scotland*, 4 vols (Edinburgh, 1907).
Larner, C, *Enemies of God* (London, 1981).
Lynch, M, *Scotland: A New History* (London, 1991).
Lynch, M (ed), *The Early Modern Town in Scotland* (London, 1987).
McAdam, D, *Edinburgh: A Landscape Fashioned by Geology* (British Geological Survey for Scottish Natural Heritage, Battleby, 1993).
MacGibbon, D & Ross, T, *Castellated and Domestic Architecture of Scotland from the Twelfth to the Eighteenth Century*, 5 vols (Edinburgh, 1887–92).

MacGibbon, D & Ross, T, *Ecclesiastical Architecture of Scotland*, 3 vols (Edinburgh, 1897).
Macinnes, A, *Charles I and the Making of the Covenanting Movement* (Edinburgh, 1991).
Mackay, A K, *Parochial School of Dalkeith* (no place, 1969).
Mackay, J A, *The History of the Burgh of Kilmarnock and of Loudon District* (Kilmarnock, 1992).
McWilliam, C, *The Buildings of Scotland: Lothian except Edinburgh*, (London, 1978).
Maxfield, V A, 'Excavations at Eskbank, Midlothian, 1972', *PSAS*, 105 (1972–4), 141–50.
Maxwell, G S, *The Romans in Scotland* (Edinburgh, 1989).
Mitchell, A, *Political and Social Movements in Dalkeith* (no place, 1882).
Mitchison, R, *A History of Scotland* (London, 1970).
Nicholson, R, *Scotland: The Later Middle Ages* (Edinburgh, 1989).
Nicolaisen, W F H, *Scottish Place-names: Their Study and Significance* (London, 1976).
Paterson, J, *History of the Regality of Musselburgh* (Musselburgh, 1861).
Perry, D *et al*, 'Excavations at Castle Park, Dunbar: 1988–90' (SUAT, forthcoming).
Pryde, G S, *Scotland from 1603 to the Present Day* (London, 1962).
Royal Commission on the Ancient and Historical Monuments of Scotland, National Monuments Record for Scotland.
Royal Commission on the Ancient and Historical Monuments of Scotland, *Tenth Report with Inventory of Monuments and Constructions in the Counties of Midlothian and West Lothian* (Edinburgh, 1929).
RSMC(D), *Robert Smith, 1722–1777, Dalkeith to Philadelphia* (Edinburgh, 1982).
Raisen, P & Rees, T, 'Excavations of three cropmark sites at Melville Nurseries, Dalkeith', *Glasgow Archaeological Journal*, 19 (1994–5), 31–50.
Rait, R & Pryde, G S, *Scotland* (London, 1954).
Sissons, J B, *The Geomorphology of the British Isles: Scotland* (London, 1976).
Skene, W F, *Celtic Scotland*, 3 vols (Edinburgh, 1886).
Smith, A, The excavation of Neolithic, Bronze Age and Early Historic features near Ratho, Edinburgh', *PSAS*, 125 (1995), 69–138.
Smout, T C, *A Century of the Scottish People* (London, 1987).
Smout, T C, *A History of the Scottish People* (London, 1969).
Stevenson, D, *The Scottish Revolution* (Newton Abbot, 1973).
Stewart, A F, *Dalkeith: Its Castle and Palace* (Edinburgh, 1925).
Thomas, J, *Midlothian: An Illustrated Architectural Guide* (Edinburgh, 1995).
Whyte, I D, 'The occupational structure of Scottish burghs in the late seventeenth century', in M Lynch (ed), *The Early Modern Town in Scotland* (London, 1987).
Whyte, I D, 'Urbanization in early-modern Scotland: a preliminary analysis', *Scottish Economic and Social History*, ix (1989).
Wickham-Jones, C, *Scotland's First Settlers* (London, 1994).
Whittow, J, *Geology and Scenery in Britain* (London, 1992).

cartographic sources

SRO RHP 562/8 'Plan of property adjacent to the road leading to the bridge over the South Esk', 1767.
SRO RHP 9520 'Plan of lands of the Duchess of Buccleuch at Dalkeith', Mr Laude, 1718.
SRO RHP 9529 'Sectional plan of the proposed alteration of road, including bridge, at Cowbridge', nd.
SRO RHP 9554 'Plan of site of proposed lodge at the Edinburgh Gate of Dalkeith', 1848.
SRO RHP 42209 'Plan of existing and proposed new road through the Marquis of Lothian's ground near Dalkeith', 1784.
SRO RHP 43214 'Plan and elevation of the bridge over the North Esk', 1760?.
Moir, D G (ed), *Early Maps of Scotland*, 2 vols (Edinburgh, 1973).
'Fifteenth Century Scottish Chart', in A Thomson, *Coldingham: Parish and Priory* (Galashiels, 1908).
'Map of eastern Scotland, including basins of Don, Dee, Tay, Forth and Tweed', by R Gordon of Straloch, *c* 1630.

'Lothian and Linlitqvo', by J Blaeu, *Atlas Novus* (Amsterdam, 1654).
'Map of Midlothian', by J Adair, 1682.
'A plan of the County of Midlothian', by J Laurie, 1763.
'A Plan of Edinburgh and Place adjacent', by J Laurie, 1766.
'Plan of Dalkeith', by John Lesslie, *c* 1770.
'A Map of the Three Lothians', by A & M Armstrong, 1773.
'Map of the Shire of Edinburgh', by J Knox, 1812.
'Edinburghshire', by J Thomson, 1821/2.
'A Plan of Dalkeith', by J Wood, 1822.
'A Map of the County of Edinburgh', by T Sharp, C Greenwood & W Fowler, 1828.
'Dalkeith and its Environs', Ordnance Survey, 1853.
Ordnance Survey 1:10,000, 1995.
Ordnance Survey 1:2,500, 1995.

index

pp 105–111

D

general index